TIM BELL'S

WHOLESALE

FLIGHT PLAN

A Step by Step Guide to Successful Real Estate Wholesaling in the 21st Century

Published by FBO Books

TIM BELL'S

WHOLESALE FLIGHT PLAN

A Step by Step Guide to Successful Real Estate Wholesaling in the 21st century

CONTENTS

INTRODUCTION

The world has changed. And so has real estate investment. Three primary factors (and others) have caused this change: The advent and common usage of personal computer devices accessing the Internet, the current appalling return on traditional passive investments (such as Certificates of Deposit and Treasury Securities) and the proliferation of real estate reality TV shows have combined to create this change. As a result, there are more real estate Investors in the marketplace now than there have ever been. But don't let that fact discourage you! In this book I'm going to show you a strategy that will allow you to take advantage of the fact that there are lots of Investors in the market now. As a Wholesaler, all of those "Fix and Flip" Investors and "Buy and Hold" Investors, desperate to find properties, become your customers.

In order to be successful as a 21st century real estate Investor, you must adopt tactics that allow you to find and secure the properties that the other Investors are looking for but can't find. That, coupled with other ideas, is what this book is all about.

Some people ask me why I call my method 'The Wholesale Flight Plan'. They ask, "What do flying and real estate investing have in common?" I have been flying airplanes since I was 16 years old. To the best of my recollection, I have flown 17 different types of aircraft; everything from a Hughes 500 helicopter and a Schweitzer sailplane, to my late cousin David's wild, aerobatic Starduster Two home built biplane. While very young, I learned to use flight plans and checklists as part of my flight training. Pilots use flight plans as planning, safety and accountability tools. If a pilot files a flight plan and doesn't arrive at his destination within a reasonable period of time, the FAA will send search crews to look for him. By filing a flight plan he is letting others know of his intentions, and he will get help if he doesn't show up at his destination. The typical flight plan is detailed enough to assist the pilot's rescuers in finding him. It includes aircraft identification information, number of people on board, proposed route of flight, destination, estimated airspeed, cruising altitude, estimated time enroute, amount of fuel on board, alternative airports and other important information. Use of this planning tool insures that the pilot has thought out and planned his flight, and that he knows where he is going and how he is going to get there. It is important in your real estate investment business for you to plan, to know where you are going and how you are going to get to your destination.

Pilots also use checklists to make sure that they don't forget to do anything important, like put the landing gear down before they land, or switch the fuel tanks before the engines run out of fuel. In fact, the airlines are so adamant that checklists be used (for everyone's safety) that they pay millions of dollars each year in salaries to pilots to read and implement those checklists. Airline pilots regularly read and follow checklists as they perform the various functions involved in flying a complex modern airliner. They have a checklist for everything from pre-start to shutting down an airplane.

As a result of this type of training and mental conditioning, I have adopted a step by step, checklist approach to many aspects of my life, including real estate investment. This book is all about my step by step, checklist approach to an incredibly exciting and profitable real estate investment strategy, commonly called 'Wholesaling.' If you diligently follow the steps that I am about to reveal to you, it is inevitable that you will do a real estate deal... it can't be avoided. You will be successful!

WHOLESALING BASICS

Imagine that you are flying along in an airliner on a trip to your favorite destination. Maybe you even purchased a first class ticket. (By the way if you've never flown in first class, I don't recommend you try it, unless you can afford to do so from now on. Once you sit up front, you'll never again be able to tolerate the "cattle car" seating and lack of service in the back!)

Again, imagine that you've just finished a wonderful meal and now you're sipping champagne from a real crystal flute. As you enjoy the luxurious, spacious ambiance of the first class cabin, it occurs to you that you've never seen the cockpit of an airliner. You ring the flight attendant and tell her that you would like to take a quick look at the cockpit and say hello to the pilots. She looks you over and says, "Well, you don't look like a terrorist; OK go knock on the door and say hello to the pilots." You knock on the cockpit door, open it and look down at the two seats, expecting to greet the pilots. But there's no one there; the seats are empty…there's no one flying the plane!

Now, if this happened to you, what are the chances that you would land safely at your destination as you anticipated you would when you boarded that plane earlier that day? Slim to none, right? A wholesale deal is like an airplane flight. It takes a certain amount of knowledge, skill, guidance and direction to come to a safe and profitable conclusion. That said, I'm going to share with you everything you need to accomplish that worthwhile goal and have that great payday.

What is Real Estate Wholesaling?

Wholesaling is defined as an Investor to Investor transaction, but can also involve selling to a quasi-retail Buyer like a mom and pop homeowner.

It is always an "A to B to C" transaction, with "A" representing the Seller, "B" representing you as the Wholesaler, and "C" representing the end Buyer. Below is a diagram of a wholesale deal. Carefully studying the diagram below will help you understand how it works.

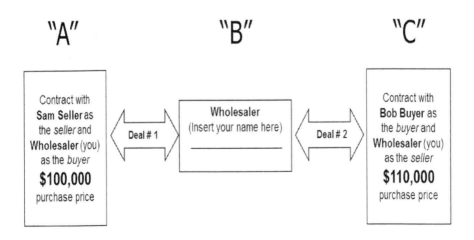

There are two essential rules of successful wholesaling:

Rule #1: The deal you structure must be a good deal for the next person (person "C", the end Buyer of the property). If it is not a good deal for them, they simply won't show up to buy it!

Rule #2: In creating a good deal for the next person, you must also include a profit for yourself.

In following my step by step, checklist approach and properly applying Rule #1, it is important to consider the question, "Who will be the most likely Buyer for my property?" If we can figure out who the Buyer will be, then we can ideally determine their criteria. If we know their criteria and the parameters they use to determine whether or not a particular deal is a good one for them, it is much more likely that we can create a deal that will be acceptable to them.

Our Buyer will be one of three types of purchasers:

Fix & Flip Rehabber Investor: This is a person who buys physically distressed properties, fixes them up and then resells them on a retail basis for a profit.

Buy & Hold Landlord Investor: This person buys properties which may or may not be physically distressed, fixes them on a minimal basis to make them livable/rentable, and then rents out the property for positive cash flow, tax benefits, principle reduction and market appreciation.

Family Home Buyer: This person buys a property which is physically distressed, fixes the property up, and then moves into it and uses the property as their primary residence.

Each of these three potential Buyers has different criteria to help them determine whether or not a particular deal is a good one for them. You never really know for sure who your Buyer will be, so I strongly suggest that you structure your deal to fit the person with the most stringent criteria. In other words, the formula of the Buyer who is typically willing to pay the least amount of money for the property is our primary target. In this way, you will automatically create a deal that is acceptable to the other two Buyer types. This keeps our "Buyer pool" as large as possible, giving us the best chance to sell the property and make our wholesale fee.

Generally speaking, the Fix & Flip Rehabber Investor uses a 70% rule analysis process, which I will go over below. These Buyers will typically pay the least amount of money for a property.

The Buy & Hold Landlord Investor will typically pay about 10% or so more for the property than a Fix & Flip Rehabber Investor because he is not looking for a big profit up front from the sale of the property. After all, he is not going to sell it, he is going to rent it out and get his profit more gradually over the time of his ownership.

The Family Home Buyer may consider the After Repair Value and the cost of repairs in determining their price, but there are often intangible emotional factors involved. For example, they may want to purchase the property because it's considered trendy or fashionable to live in the area. Or maybe it is in the old neighborhood where they grew up and they want to move back in to be near their friends and relatives. Plus, Family Home Buyers typically plan to do the work on the property themselves, which skews their consideration of repair costs. Most Fix & Flip Investors and Buy & Hold Investors hire professional contractors to do the work on the property, rather than do it themselves. Most Family Home Buyers only consider their ability to qualify for a loan, or the amount of cash they have available, when they decide how much they will pay for a property. These people will therefore typically pay the most for the property of the three Buyer types listed.

Since the Fix & Flip Rehabber will typically pay the least amount of money for a property, his criteria becomes our target for following Rule #1. If we can structure a deal so that it is a good deal for him, it will almost always be a good deal for the other two Buyer types.

The bottom line is this: It is critical that we focus on the needs and desires of our best potential Buyers, the Fix & Flip Investors and the Buy & Hold Investors. If we keep their needs in mind we will always create a deal that is acceptable to them and they will be more likely to come and buy it from us, and we will therefore get paid!

Here is a sample of the 70% rule calculations that a typical Fix & Flip Investor will use. The numbers will vary from market to market and from property to property, but the percentages and principles will remain essentially the same.

$200,000	After Repair Value (abbreviated as "ARV", aka the sales price after rehab)
-$ 20,000	General Costs (Holding, Loan, Carrying and Sales Costs typically about 10% of ARV)
-$ 40,000	Profit (typically 20% of ARV)
-$ 30,000	Repair/Rehab costs (not a function of the ARV)
$110,000	Maximum Purchase Price for a Fix & Flip Investor

To summarize, if, as in our example above, the Fix and Flip Rehabber Investor can buy the property at $110,000, fix it for $30,000 and resell it at $200,000, he will walk away with a check from his title company or title attorney for $40,000. This property priced at $110,000 then represents a good deal for him. We now know the appropriate price on this property to satisfy Rule #1.

We now subtract the amount of profit we wish to make in order to satisfy Rule #2.

$200,000	After Repair Value ("ARV", Sales Price after rehab)
-$ 20,000	General Costs (Holding, Loan, Carrying and Sales Costs about 10% of ARV)
-$ 40,000	Profit (20% of ARV)
-$ 30,000	Repair/Rehab costs
$110,000	Maximum Purchase Price for Fix and Flip Rehabber Investor
- $10,000	Wholesaler's profit or Wholesaler's fee
$100,000	Wholesaler's maximum contract offer price to the Seller

At $100,000 as our agreed upon purchase price with the Seller, our deal now meets the requirements of both Rule #1 and Rule #2.

Our next step is to negotiate a contract sales price of $100,000 or less with the Seller of the property, which we will discuss in detail in later chapters.

Note: All of the numbers used above are for illustration purposes and may have little resemblance to reality in your marketplace. That said, the formula is sound. We will discuss how to calculate all the numbers in the above formula later. Also, people often ask me what 'percentage' I use to calculate the wholesale fee. In real life, real world application of these principles there is no 'percentage' used to calculate your wholesale fee. Your wholesale fee is simply the difference between what the Buyer will pay (based on his formula) and what the Seller will accept (based on his motivation.) Put indelicately, your wholesale fee is whatever you can get away with!

Exit Strategies

We will now skip ahead to your potential exit strategies for your deal. Don't worry; we will go over everything in between in subsequent chapters. For now, assume that you have the property under your contractual control by virtue of your agreement with the Seller.

There is an old saying amongst military and police officers, "Know your exit before you enter." In other words you should know how you're going to get out of a potentially hazardous situation before you get into a potentially hazardous situation. This concept also applies to a wholesale deal. As a consequence we're going to discuss exit strategies right now. I have found that if you are thoroughly familiar with the 'end game' you are attempting to play, it is much more likely that you'll be able to put it together and make it happen, and therefore profit in your wholesale deal. Also, your wholesale deal will often involve several other people, namely, a Seller, a Buyer, a title company or title attorney and others. If you don't understand the process from start to finish, it is unlikely that you'll be able to explain various parts of the process, when necessary, to the other people in involved in your deal. Finally, it is traditional for real estate agents to act in the role of "Cruise Director" in a real estate transaction, assuring that all the people and parts come together in a timely fashion, as appropriate. They typically do this because they are the only ones in the transaction that understand all of the components. Also, guiding the transaction along helps to assure that they will get a paycheck. As I said before, if there's no one "flying the plane" it's most likely going to crash. In my unofficial, unscientific observation over my 38 years in real estate investment, only about 3% of the real estate agents in North America understand the concept of wholesaling. Also, in many cases, you may not have a real estate agent involved in your transaction at all, especially if you're dealing directly with the Seller. For all of these reasons, I feel it is important that you clearly understand the available exit strategies for your wholesale deal.

You recall our previous wholesale deal diagram:

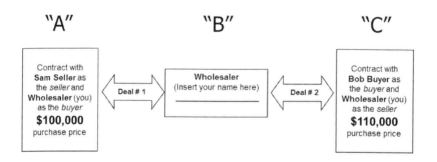

There are 3 suggested ways to exit these two deals and make a profit:

1. Assignment of contract

2. Simultaneous closing (also known as a double closing)

3. Transactional funding

Which of these strategies you use depends upon the nature of the deal you strike with the Seller and the Buyer. If you use Assignment of Contract, the Buyer will know everything about the contract you created with the Seller, including the price. In many cases that is OK, but in some circumstances it may not be OK. For example, if your wholesale fee would seem to be inappropriate to the Buyer (too high) it may be best to use one of the other two exit strategies. Exit strategies two and three should be used any time you feel it desirable to "mask" or "hide" the contract price with the Seller, the contract price with the Buyer, and/or your wholesale fee. There will be other times when Assignment of Contract will not work, such as a bank owned property, or a short sale property. Banks will not typically allow your contract with them to be assignable, so you must use a different strategy.

There is another really obvious strategy, but I generally don't discuss it because most people that I talk to cannot use it or don't want to use it. Obviously, you could purchase the Seller's property with your own cash, and then immediately turn around and resell it to the Buyer. There are two reasons that I usually don't recommend this exit strategy. Number one, most people don't have the cash to purchase the property upfront, and number two, even if you do have the cash to purchase the property, your wholesale fee would be significantly eroded by the costs of closing two separate deals. So let's move on the exit strategies that I *do* recommend.

1) Assignment of Contract (See Diagram Below)

You simply assign your interest in your contract with Sam Seller to Bob Buyer for a fee of $10,000. When he "buys" your contract with Sam, Bob purchases the right to buy the property at $100,000. Bob is typically OK with that because he stands to make a $40,000 profit if he buys into the deal at $110,000. You and Bob sign an "Assignment of Contract" form in front of a notary, you give Bob your original contract with Sam, and Bob gives you $10,000. Bob goes on to close with Sam and you go out and spend your $10,000.

YOUR PROFIT: $10,000

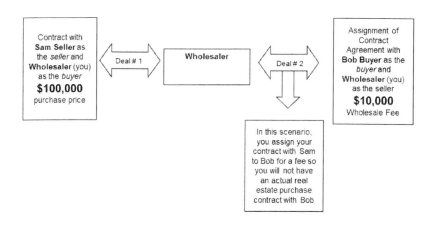

2) Simultaneous or Double Closing (See Diagram Below)

You meet with Bob at 10:00 am on the day of closing at the title company. You sign the paperwork as the Seller of the property and Bob signs the paperwork as the Buyer of the property AND brings in his check for $110,000. Tammy Title, the title officer, directs this process and then gathers all the paperwork from this closing together and places it in a file folder. You and Bob shake hands and leave the title company.

At 1:00 pm that same day, you return to the title company to close with Sam. Sam signs the Seller's documents and you sign the Buyer's documents as directed by Tammy the title officer. You and Sam shake hands and both leave the title company. Then Tammy the title officer places the paperwork from your closing with Sam in another file folder.

At 4:00 pm that afternoon, Tammy the title officer instructs her runner, Jimmy, to take both files to the county recorder's office. Jimmy is instructed to record the two deals in the opposite order in which they were actually signed and closed. This is acceptable because there is no time stamp on the title officer's notarization of the documents, only a date stamp. Jimmy the runner records your deal with Sam first, and then a minute or so later records your deal with Bob. This makes perfect sense to the clerk at the recorder's office and is perfectly acceptable to them, and so they record the two deals.

The next day you go to the title company and pick up your check, as does Sam Seller. Bob Buyer gets the keys to the property and everyone is happy.

YOUR PROFIT: $34,000 ($40,000 minus $6,000 in closing costs you owe to the title company)

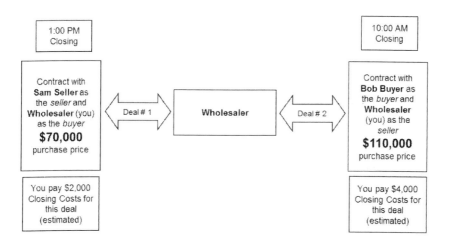

3) Transactional Funding (See Diagram Below)

You send a copy of the contract for Deal #1 between you and Sam Seller, and a copy of the contract for Deal #2 between you and Bob Buyer to Scott Bigbucks at USA Private Money, a Transactional Funding company. Scott looks over the contracts, sees that they are legitimate and reasonable, and then wire transfers $70,000 to Tammy Title's escrow account to be earmarked for your closing with Sam. Along with the money, Scott sends detailed escrow instructions. Those instructions indicate that Scott's $70,000 is to be released to fund your transaction with Sam ONLY if you and Sam show up and sign AND you and Bob show up and sign (and of course, Bob must bring his $110,000, too.) If and only if all these things happen, then Tammy has Scott's permission to fund Deal #1 on your behalf, just as though you had shown up with cash.

Of course, no lender does anything for free, and Scott Bigbucks at USA Private Money is no exception. Transactional Funding fees vary amongst lenders, but he will typically charge 2-3% of the amount borrowed, even though this closing process typically only takes a day or two at the most.

YOUR PROFIT: $31,900 ($40,000 minus $6,000 in closing costs you owe to the title company and minus $2,100 you owe the Transactional Funding Company)

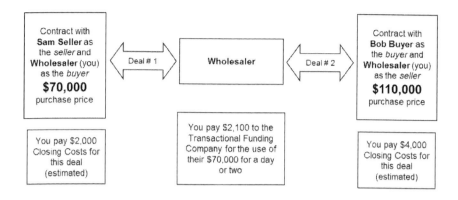

Step Two

IDENTIFYING YOUR FOCUS NEIGHBORHOODS

Wholesale deals are everywhere. They can be found in any price range and in every neighborhood. That said, I don't recommend that you start out in the gated multimillion dollar golf course community by the lake. Conversely I also think that you should not start in what we call the "war zone." These are neighborhoods characterized by random gunfire, lots of graffiti, a lot of the yellow police "do not cross this line" tape and chalk outlines of dead bodies on the sidewalks. It is important to remember that regardless of your exit strategy someone must be willing and able to live in the house on which you create a wholesale deal. If the house is in an expensive neighborhood hardly anyone can afford to buy it which means that your audience for that particular property is very small, reducing the likelihood that it will sell quickly. If your house is in the really bad neighborhood then people can afford it but no one wants to live there. We need to focus on neighborhoods that are somewhere in between. By the way a neighborhood consists of somewhere between 50 and 300 homes. Another name for it might be a subdivision (or two.) If you focus on an entire city or entire county then your marketing efforts may be too diluted.

Ultimately we are looking for neighborhoods that are economically somewhere between the most expensive and the least expensive. The best place to look is in neighborhoods that are at, slightly below, or slightly above the *median sold price for single family homes* in your entire marketplace. A good way to gauge the suitability of a neighborhood for your wholesale business is to look at several additional factors, too.

Neighborhoods that are predominantly three bedroom, two bath houses will be the most attractive to your Fix & Flip Investor Buyers, and your Buy & Hold Investor Buyers. In most markets three bedroom two bath homes are the most saleable and desirable. Also most Buy & Hold Landlord Investors find that three bedroom two bath houses are the easiest to rent.

Another important characteristic is that of low Days On Market. *Days On Market* is a jargon term that real estate agents and appraisers use to describe how long it takes to sell a home. Average Days On Market takes into account the sales of all the homes in a particular neighborhood or city or MLS marketplace. Also it is important to note that Days On Market is a relative term. In some markets in North America, 20 or 30 days is a relatively high Days On Market figure because homes that are selling quickly sell in 7 to 10 days. In other markets 90 days is considered fast because the average Days On Market is somewhere between 120 in 180 days. Average Days On Market is an important metric to us as Wholesalers, mostly because it is very important to our wholesale Buyers. If you ever watch any of the real estate reality TV shows you will notice that the principals, the Investors, are always fanatically focused on selling the property as quickly as possible. If they suffer any delays such as a contractor are telling them they can't get the job done on time, or a delay in the closing because of something the agent or the Buyer does, they are always upset. Then it's drama, drama and more drama. The truth is that Fix & Flip Investors and, to a lesser degree, Buy & Hold Investors, are always interested in getting the property done as quickly as possible. It is universally acknowledged that holding costs on a fix and flip property, if they extend over an unexpected or inappropriate period of time, can significantly erode the profit of the Investor. Consequently we want to focus on neighborhoods where things are moving quickly, where people are coming and going, where properties are being bought and sold at as rapid a pace as possible. This will make those neighborhoods, and specifically those properties, very attractive to our wholesale Buyers.

Actually, low Days On Market is a quick and easy shortcut to finding the most desirable neighborhoods in your marketplace for Fix & Flip Investors. Ask your real estate agent to help you identify those neighborhoods where things are moving quickly. They can typically do this in the statistical analysis portion of their MLS Computer System data. Occasionally, when I mention the idea of looking for fast moving neighborhoods, some people question that concept. They say things to me like, "Won't that mean that I'm competing with everyone else in a hot neighborhood?" Yes, however you're going to use somewhat unorthodox finding methods that other people either don't know about or are not willing to use, thereby reducing or eliminating your competition (we'll get to those in Chapter 3.)

The last thing I want to mention in regards to choosing your focus neighborhoods is physical proximity to you. I generally recommend that you structure your real estate business so that it is relatively convenient, especially if you have other commitments on your time such as a job, family commitments, community commitments or other obligations. I suggest that you focus on neighborhoods that are within approximately a 30 minute driving radius of where you live or were you work. That would mean a maximum of a 1 hour trip to and from a property to check it out. In many years of training people to invest in real estate I have found that if you stay within the 30 minute one way driving radius or the 1 hour roundtrip radius you will be less likely to procrastinate checking out properties. Obviously if you procrastinate looking at properties you're basically procrastinating your real estate investment business and therefore putting off your success. Taking action with the information I'm providing for you is the most important component for your success in your real estate investment business, so obviously procrastinating is not acceptable.

There are however some exceptions to the 30 minute driving radius rule. The first exception would be if you live in a highly urbanized area such as Los Angeles. If you have ever driven in rush hour traffic near a big city like Los Angeles you recognize that you may only go ½ mile in a 30 minute time frame. You may need to go outside of the 30 minute driving radius for a highly urbanized area in order to get to the more affordable homes. The other exception is if you live in a very rural area. If the small rural town that you live in has 523 souls living there, frankly, there are just not enough houses for you to do business with. You may have to go farther than a 30 minute driving radius just to find enough houses to give you the opportunity you're looking for.

Once you have identified 2 to 6 neighborhoods that have the characteristics we've discussed then it's a great idea to get a map of those areas and look at the layout of the streets and the neighborhood. If you are uncertain about a particular neighborhood I highly recommend that you check it out virtually by looking at it on Google Maps. Use Google's aerial photo views and also street views to look around the neighborhoods and get a feel for what is there. Once you are satisfied that the neighborhoods look acceptable on Google Maps then get in your car and drive the neighborhoods, up and down each street. You should look for and take note of all of the vacant properties, all of the run down, nasty, ugly, bad properties, all the properties with for sale by owner signs in front, and all the properties that have real estate agent's signs in the yard.

Now that you're going out into the neighborhoods it's time to talk about how to find the owner of a vacant property and also what to say to the Seller of any property. First let's talk about how to find the owner of a vacant property. Below is a list of several different things you can do to find the owner of a vacant property.

While you are in the neighborhood contact the neighbors, two on the left, two on the right and five across the street. Put a big smile on your face, pull out your business card and knock on the door. Introduce yourself, tell them you are interested in buying their neighbor's vacant home, and ask if they know how to reach them. Sometimes, when people abandon a property, they leave contact information with some of the neighbors just in case of an emergency. If they know how to reach the person, collect the information and thank them. If they don't know how to reach the person, thank them anyway and ask them if they know anyone else in the neighborhood who is thinking about moving. In some cases this will be enough information to help you find the owner.

Next, you may want to look up the owner's name and other information in the county records. As of this writing my favorite source of the availability of county records is Netronline.com, but of course as fast as technology changes you may need to find another source. Once you find the owner's name, you may be able to find them on some kind of an online database search program such as Zabasearch.com. Of course these types of resources are constantly changing and you may need to look up and find what is the most current method of searching for people on the Internet today. Once you determine who the owner is, you may want to call the 411 information operator to see if a new number has been issued to that person recently.

If you still can't find them, consider sending a letter like the one in Exhibit 1 in the Appendix in the back of the book or, if you find an alternative mailing address in the county property records, you can certainly send the letter there, too.

If you still can't find the owner consider placing a sign on the property. You may or may not have heard of the idea of a bandit sign. My current favorite bandit sign looks like this:

```
┌─────────────────────────────┐
│                             │
│       CALL ME ABOUT         │
│        THIS HOUSE!          │
│                             │
│       801-555-1212          │
│                             │
└─────────────────────────────┘
```

When you place this sign on the private property portion of the house (typically on the front lawn) be prepared to receive calls. Some of the calls that you receive will not be from the owner of the property but from a potential Buyer asking you for information about the property. If you have yet to contact the owner when one of these folks calls, simply tell them that you haven't acquired all the details on the property but that you anticipate that you will soon, and ask them if they would like you to call them when you have that information. They always say "yes." Collect their phone number and agree to call them back.

In most cases you will receive a call from the owner of the property. When handling these calls it is important that you follow a particular process. About 50% of the time when the Seller calls, they will express confusion and say things like, "I'm not sure why your sign is on my property, I'm a little confused, did your sign company place it on the wrong property?" The other half of the time they will express anger saying things like, "Why did you put your sign on my property, that's not your property that's my property?" Regardless of what they express, confusion or anger, your answer will always be the same. It's a simple three step process.

Step number one, a profuse apology. Step number two, a profuse thank you. Step number three, ask if they want to sell their house. Here is how your dialog might sound:

"Mr. Seller I'm so sorry for putting that sign up on your property...Please forgive me. I've been trying to find you and couldn't, so in desperation I put that sign up on your property in hopes that you would call me, and you did. Thank you so much for calling me! The reason I want to talk with you is that I want to buy your house. Would you like to sell it?"

If you say it fast and don't slow down or allow them to interrupt you, it will work great. I will address the script to use after they say "yes" or "no" next, but first lets go over the final finding method.

If, after using all the above Seller-finding methods, you still have not found the owner, I suggest that you purchase an online skip trace, which, at the time of this writing, will cost you about $25.00. Sometimes when I suggest that someone spend $25.00 to find the owner of a vacant property I get some raised eyebrows and they tell me that it sounds expensive. By the time I've gone through all the other finding methods and still haven't found the Seller, I typically get excited. If I've tried everything else and I still can't find the Seller it is usually worth the $25.00 to find them because I know that no one else has been able to find them. Most Investors give up after using only one or two of the methods that I've mentioned. I know that if I persist and follow through I will most likely make a lot of money on that house because there's no one else competing with me for it!

My current favorite online skip trace company is www.findtheseller.com but you can use anyone that you like.

If you will persist and implement all the methods I've mentioned you will find your share of Sellers and put "competition free" deals together.

Now it's time to talk about the script that you can use with the Seller of a property. I believe strongly in being scripted with most of the things I say to potential Sellers and Buyers. If you're scripted it will reduce your anxiety and help you focus and stay on track in your conversations with Sellers and Buyers. Realize that you don't need to memorize the script. It's OK to print it off and take it with you. That said, do your best to familiarize yourself with your script so it comes out naturally when talking with a potential Seller.

Please see the Seller Script in Exhibit 2 in the Appendix. If you read it carefully you'll notice that there is one introductory portion for a telephone call and another introductory portion for an in-person, face to face visit. If you will simply follow this script you'll be amazed at the amount of success that you will have talking with Sellers. Eventually you will feel relaxed and at ease when you talk with them. Like anything in life, talking with Sellers gets easier the more you do it. If you will force yourself to do it initially, it will become second nature to you very soon.

If the answer to the question "do you want to sell" is yes, the information that you gather in asking these questions is critical in determining how much you should pay for that property. And that is the topic of our next chapter. We will discuss analyzing the property to determine the answer to the question, "How much is this property be worth to my Fix & Flip Investor Buyer?" and also, "How much is this property worth to *me* as a Wholesaler?"

Step Three

ANALYZING PROPERTIES

As you likely recognize your ability to analyze properties is critical to your success as a real estate Investor. As mentioned before, we want to focus on the Fix & Flip Investor's criteria, using the aforementioned formula:

$200,000	After Repair Value (abbreviated as "ARV", Sales Price after rehab)
-$ 20,000	General Costs (Holding, Loan, Carrying and Sales Costs about 10% of ARV)
-$ 40,000	Profit (20% of ARV)
-$ 30,000	Repair/Rehab costs
$110,000	Maximum Purchase Price for Fix and Flip Rehabber
- $10,000	Wholesaler's profit or Wholesaler's fee
$100,000	Wholesaler's maximum contract offer price to the Seller

If you consider this formula from a logical, mathematical perspective, it becomes very evident that it is quite simple, and that all you really need are two numbers in order to crank through and come up with your answer: the After Repair Value, and the repair cost estimate. Since the General costs (holding costs, loan costs, carrying costs, sales costs, etc.) are typically about 10% of the After Repair Value and

26

the profit that a Fix & Flip Investor builds into the deal is typically 20% of the After Repair Value, it is very easy to then calculate these two values using the After Repair Value figure. Because the General Cost amount and the Profit amount are both a function of the After Repair Value, if we have the After Repair Value and the repair cost amount, we have everything we need to complete and calculate the formula. We will start with a brief discussion of the components of the General Costs, which will be followed by a discussion of the Profit. Then we will get into the methods that you will use to calculate the After Repair Value and the Repair costs. At that point you will have everything you need to complete your formula, and you will know how much that property is worth to your Fix & Flip Investor Buyer, and how much it is worth to you as a Wholesaler.

The General or Miscellaneous costs--Closing, Holding, Carrying and Sales Costs (typically 10% or so of After Repair Value)

These costs breakdown into three specific categories. Please understand that as a Wholesaler these are *not* costs that you will incur but rather costs that your Fix & Flip Investor Buyer will incur in their fix and flip process. Remember, you always need to look at every property from your Buyer's perspective.

When someone buys a property there are always closing costs. These costs may be somewhat negotiable, but as a

Buyer, your Fix & Flip Investor should definitely take them into consideration as they will have to plan on paying at least some of them. See Exhibit 3 in the Appendix for a breakdown of these costs.

The list of general costs in the Appendix represents some typical costs generally associated with buying, holding and selling a property, but there may be others in your area. Be sure to research these costs thoroughly for your market before you buy or sell. The easiest way to do this is by checking with your local team members (real estate agent, title company, real estate attorney, mortgage loan officer, insurance agent, utility company, etc.) Be sure to get accurate estimates of these "costs" as they can vary widely from market to market. In some markets and under some loan terms, the "10%" portion of the "70% rule" may not be enough to cover those costs. Please check before you buy.

The easiest way to clearly determine these costs is to have your title company or title attorney prepare a "Proposed, Estimated or Pro Forma HUD-1 Settlement Statement." This is a document which shows all the charges involved in a real estate transaction and designates the distribution of the monies involved in that transaction to the appropriate parties. Your friendly neighborhood title person will know what you are talking about when you ask for this document by name. They will typically need some basic information on your transaction such as purchase price, estimated settlement date, loan payoff amount on the Seller's mortgage(s), Seller contribution to Buyer's closing costs, Buyer's loan amount, Buyer's down payment amount, annual property taxes and real estate commissions. Once you provide this information, they can very easily prepare this document for you. (If necessary, feel free to show this information to your title person to help them understand what you want.) Please recognize that the title company will not have information on the middle section (Holding Costs) and that you need to figure this information with the help of your utility companies, insurance agent, and lender.

The Profit (the Fix & Flip Investor Buyer's profit, *not* the Wholesaler's Profit)

A typical Fix & Flip Investor will consider approximately 20% of the After Repair Value to be an appropriate profit amount to build into their deal. This is a typical figure in most markets in North America. That said, if you live in an expensive market such as coastal California or New York City or Vancouver, British Columbia, the profit amount that a Fix & Flip Investor builds into his deal may be less. In more expensive, retail type markets 10% or so of the after repair value will generally be considered adequate for a Fix & Flip Investor's profit margin. After all if the after repair value of your property is $800,000, 10% of that or $80,000, would be considered a reasonable payday for most Fix & Flip Investors. If, on the other hand, you live in a wholesale market, such as St. Louis, Pittsburg, Detroit or Baltimore, the Fix & Flip Investors there, by virtue of the extra risk they tolerate, may expect more than a 20% of ARV profit. I know of two brothers who invest in urban Baltimore. They created a deal that fit perfectly into the standard 20% of ARV profit expectation formula. They physically showed the property to 27 different Fix & Flip Investors from two local REI clubs and got no offers. They were beside themselves. In desperation, they contacted the president of one of the local clubs and asked him why none of the 27 Investors wanted the property. They carefully went through all the numbers on their deal, and he quickly identified the problem. He said, "You're asking too much for the property." When they pointed out to him that if fit perfectly into the formula, allowing a 20% of ARV profit to the Investor, he said, "That's the problem. Investors in our market expect to make a 30% profit, not 20% profit; 20% just isn't enough to justify the risk." The brothers subsequently lowered the price to reflect a 30% profit to the Fix & Flip Investors, and sold the property for cash in 2 days. The lesson here is to confirm with the Investors in your market their expectations regarding profit.

Now we move on calculating After Repair Value and Repair Costs on any given property.

After Repair Value

Now I'm going to teach you a shortcut to determining after repair value. The traditional method of determining after repair value is to examine as many "comps" or comparable properties as possible. Sometimes finding appropriate comparable properties can be challenging. Even experienced Investors can sometimes struggle with finding the After Repair Value on a property. Often, they will look at sold properties, active listings, expired listings, and pending sales in an effort to find the After Repair Value. This of course involves a lot of time and effort and energy, and may cause you to lose a property due to the length of the examination process. Often, someone else will beat you to the property. There is an easier way!

Simply use the following dialog with your real estate agent:

Investor to Agent ARV Dialog

Ms. Agent, I am considering buying this property and fixing it up. It won't be perfect, but it will be very nice, a 9 on a scale of 1 to 10...it will look new, smell new and feel new.

If I were to buy this property, fix it up and hire you to sell it for me, how much would you be able to sell it for?

Before you answer, please recognize that I am counting on your answer to help me decide whether or not I will purchase this property. You know my formula:

$200,000	*After Repair Value (Sales Price after rehab)*
-$ 20,000	*General Costs (Holding, Sales, Carrying Costs, Etc.)*
-$ 40,000	*Our Profit*
-$ 30,000	*Repair/Rehab costs*
$110,000	*Maximum Offer For Ownership Price*

Obviously, because I am starting with the future sales price and then subtracting my costs in order to determine how much I should pay for the property, it is critical that you get it right or it could completely mess up my deal. I need a completely honest, accurate figure from you, with no fluff and no hype. I need to know how much you could actually sell it for in a relatively short period of time after I finish the remodel…30 to 60 days maximum market time. I don't really care what number you give me as long as it is accurate.

Please understand that if the figure you give me now turns out to be too high and you can't really sell the property for the price that you give me today, it is unlikely that I will work with you again because I can't afford to do unprofitable deals. I'm counting on you to "sharpen your pencil" and really "do your homework" in order to give me an accurate amount. I realize that no one can perfectly predict the future, but I'm expecting you to use your professional knowledge and experience to determine an accurate selling price.

So again I ask, **if I were to buy this property, fix it up and hire you to sell it for me, how much would you be able to sell it for?"**

Once they give you a dollar figure, ask your agent to send you the comparable properties they used to confirm and document their price. And there you have it!

Repair Cost Estimate

Now that you have the after repair value all you really need is the repair cost estimate in order to complete your calculations. Repair costs can either be estimated by you or by your contractor. However, there is a problem with asking your contractor to meet you at the property to give you an estimate. Unless your contractor is your brother in law, or you saved his life during the war and he owes you a big favor, after looking at somewhere between 5 to 10 properties together and giving you his written estimate, he will stop returning your calls! Think about it from his perspective. You keep asking him to come to properties, spend 20 to 60 minutes of his working time to give you an estimate, but you never hire him to do any work! This is a sure way to burn out your contractor. Once you've burned out one contractor, you'll have to find another to give you estimates, and another, and another. Realize, of course, that you won't be able to get all of the properties that you make offers on. In fact, you won't get *most* of the properties that you make offers on. Typically, you will need to make offers on somewhere between 25 to 50 homes before you have one acceptable deal. If each contractor tolerates giving you five written estimates without being hired, you would need to have 5 to 10 contractors just to get your first offer accepted. At that rate, you will quickly run of contractors in your town to give you estimates. There is a better way. You can estimate the rehab costs by simply calculating a cost per square foot for repairs based on the amount of work that needs to be done on the property.

In nearly 40 years of real estate I have never seen two properties that needed the same amount of rehab. They are all different! Even if they were built in the same year, by the same builder, with the same floor plan, in the same neighborhood, no two houses are in the same condition. As a result, there are a million shades of gray when it comes to estimating rehab costs on a property. I suggest that the best technique is to simplify your repair estimate analysis by categorizing any property in only one of four categories:

Small PaintPlus includes paint, flooring, minor landscaping, some interior and exterior details, and a good, thorough cleaning.

Medium PaintPlus includes all of the above, plus a Kitchen and Bathroom(s).

Large PaintPlus includes all of the above plus 2 "Big Ticket" items such as roof repair or replacement, new siding, new guttering, major systems repair or replacement, such as, HVAC, plumbing, electrical, sewer, foundation, structural, etc., major landscaping and major additions.

Extra Large PaintPlus includes the Light and Medium items plus 4 "Big Ticket" items listed above.

Some people ask, "Why do all levels of remodel include everything listed in the Small PaintPlus remodel category?" A Fix & Flip Investor should always do paint and flooring and cleaning in every property, period.

If you think about it, paint and flooring cover 85% to 95% of all the surfaces in a property. If you cover the walls and the ceilings with fresh paint, and you renew the flooring (with carpet, wood, or tile) you have renewed the majority of the surfaces in that home. All that's left are the cabinets, the countertops, the plumbing fixtures and the appliances. This means that you have improved the look of the majority of the surfaces in the property. Also, ironically, paint and flooring are typically the least expensive things you can do to make the property look and feel renewed.

A survey I once saw showed that a large majority of Americans have a positive emotional response to "new car smell." You know, that smell that eminates from that fresh-from-the-factory car sitting on the dealer's showroom floor. "New car smell" comes from the materials that were used to manufacture the car: various types of plastics, vinyl, leather, metal, electronics, rubber and some lubricants. The vapors that emanate from these materials are the source of what we know as "new car smell."

Just as there is such a thing as "new car smell" there is also such a thing as "new house smell. "New house smell" comes primarily from the vapors that emanate from fresh paint and new flooring. So, by renewing these surfaces with fresh paint and flooring, we not only make them look better but they also smell better, which can be a big influencing factor for many Buyers.

The illustration in Exhibit 4 in the Appendix shows you how to quickly estimate remodeling costs. Remember this is only a rough estimate and is not exact. It is what my college physics professor used to call a S.W.A.G., a Scientific Wild Ass Guess. As a Wholesaler, a good guess is just fine for us.

Why? Because our Fix & Flip Investor Buyer will not trust our estimate of the rehab costs anyway! He will always do his own due diligence. In fact, he will verify every figure that we have given him regarding this property to make sure that it is accurate and that it fits into his formula.

When I was a kid, my friends used to have a saying, "Close counts in horseshoes and hand grenades." This saying referred, of course, to the fact that you don't have to get a "ringer" every time in throwing horseshoes because you get some points for just getting close to the post. Also, if you throw a hand grenade anywhere near your target, when it explodes it is going to do some damage. The point being that you don't have to be exact, you just have to be close. **Well, close counts in Wholesaling, too.**

The simple truth of Wholesaling is that the market will tell you whether or not you have correctly priced the property. In our current marketplace (and I don't mean the marketplace in New York or Los Angeles or Seattle or Miami, I mean the marketplace in the entirety of *North America*) if you price a wholesale property properly, it will sell, period. As I mentioned before there are many Fix & Flip Investors and Buy & Hold Investors that are looking for properties, and if you can be their supplier you will always have a ready market, eager to purchase your good deals. My rule of thumb is, when in doubt, put it under contract, and offer it to the market, and see what happens. The market will tell you whether or not you have priced the property correctly. If, for example, you go into a shoe store you may see a wonderful pair of shoes, and you would love to buy them. If you turn them over and see that the price is way too high, you simply put them down and walk away. The same thing can happen with your wholesale property. If your Buyer cannot see the value in the property that you're offering them, they simply won't buy it. That is the reason why it is so critical that we create a deal that represents a good deal for our Buyer.

Step Four

50 WAYS TO FIND PROPERTIES

Finding properties is the lifeblood of your real estate investment business. If you don't find properties, you don't have anything to analyze, you don't have anything to negotiate over, you don't have anything to buy, and you don't have anything to sell. Without finding properties you don't really have a real estate investment business, you just have a dream.

So now I'm going to talk about 50 different ways to find properties. These are certainly not the only ways to find properties but this is a very comprehensive list that has been compiled over many years.

There are several ways to use this list of finding methods. Some people treat it like a buffet restaurant. A buffet restaurant has all different types of food, but no matter how hungry they are, no one eats *everything* at the buffet. You pick and choose the things that you like, the things that are appetizing to you. You might, for example, take the prime rib and leave the halibut; you might take the broccoli and leave the green beans; you might take the chocolate pudding and leave the vanilla ice cream for dessert. You only pick and choose the things that you like and don't take the things that you don't like. That is one way to use this list of 50 ways to find properties. Choose the things that are appealing and appetizing to you and then implement those.

Another way to decide which method you will use could be based on cost or time. I will tell you that some of the items listed here are outrageously expensive. For example in my marketplace a typical billboard costs approximately $3000 a month to rent. That's pretty steep to me. On the other hand, some other things on the list are entirely free. For example, it doesn't cost you anything to pick up a telephone and call someone, such as a property manager, and ask them if one of their landlord owners wants to sell one of their properties.

On the other hand, some of the methods listed are very time consuming. Driving neighborhoods looking for vacant and ugly properties can take quite a bit of time. Others take very little time at all, especially once you have them set up. For example, once you have a direct mailing setup, its relatively easy to maintain that mailing. Also, you could easily hire some one to create, manage and fulfill your mailing program, costing you no time at all. Ultimately, you may want to consider striking a balance between cost and time consumption.

Sometimes, when I share this list with driven, type "A" personalities, they say to me, " No, no, no Tim, don't tell me all of the 50 ways to find properties, just tell me the ones that work!" My response is, they all work, otherwise they wouldn't be on the list. If you're asking which ones work, you're asking the wrong question. Your question should not be "Which ones work?" but rather "Which ones *am I* going to work on?" Hopefully, this is not a revelation to you, but real estate investment, like anything else in life that will earn you a lot of money, is *work*. It is very rewarding, enjoyable work, with a flexible schedule and a ton of control over your time and your life. But it is work. So the question begs itself, what work am I going to do to find the properties I need for my wholesale real estate investment business? The answer to that question lies in the following information.

50 Ways to Find Properties

1.   **Drive your focus neighborhoods** at least 3 hours per week looking for vacant, run-down and ugly properties. For vacant properties, record the address, look up the owner and contact them (we go over how to find them later.) For occupied properties stop your car, pull out your business card, put a big smile on your face, walk right up to the door, and knock. Use the Seller Script discussed in chapter two and you're on your way to finding a property to wholesale.

2.   **Contact the Code Enforcement or Code Compliance Officer** for your focus areas. They are a part of the city government, and are tasked with finding and enforcing violations of the city building, zoning and upkeep codes. If

you think about it, the code enforcement people are really just people who are paid to drive around and find ugly and vacant properties, the same concept I suggested in method number one. The difference is that the code enforcement people are being paid by your city to look for the same properties that you are looking for. Arguably, if you pay taxes in your city, they are already on your payroll, they just don't know it yet! They have the huge benefits of being paid a salary, being provided a vehicle and gasoline, being provided with healthcare benefits, vacation days, and other perks of working for the city. Also, they have something that you will never have, and that is a hotline to City Hall. If someone calls up to complain about one of their neighbors not taking care of their property, the code enforcement officer is going to be notified, and will then make it a point to visit the property, and determine if there is a violation. In some cities, the code enforcement officer merely issues a verbal warning. In other cities they provide the violator with a letter of warning, insisting that they fix up the property within a prescribed period of time. Still other cities issue a violation, similar to a traffic ticket. The homeowner will then have 30, 60 or 90 days to eliminate the problem and demonstrate to the city that they have done so. They will also have to pay a fine, typically. If they don't pay the fine, eventually the city will issue a Lien against the property. If the Lien is not paid off within a prescribed period of time, the city could foreclose for nonpayment, and theoretically, take the property. Every city is different in regards to their techniques for enforcing the codes and punishing violators. But most cities in America today do have some form of upkeep codes and therefore code enforcement. To implement this finding method, simply introduce yourself to the code enforcement officers including the statement, "My associate Investors and I buy, fix up and resell properties to nice families…we are making America a better place to live, one home at a time…you're in favor of that, aren't you?" If they are in favor of making your city better place to live, then ask them to share the code enforcement list with you. Tell them that you will contact the homeowners and offer to buy their property. Explain that you won't tell the homeowner where you got their information. If you purchase the property, you and your partners (your wholesale Buyers) will fix up the property, move a nice new family in, and thereby, get it off the code enforcement list.

If they are reluctant to give you the list, please note that the Freedom of Information Act of 1976 requires, by Federal law, that a government entity share with you any information that they have that is not considered top secret or classified. By Federal law they must provide those records to you upon request. That said, please remember, when dealing with code enforcement people, and other municipal employees, you catch more flies with honey than you do with vinegar. Befriending the code enforcement officer is always the best approach.

3. **Contact glass companies, restoration services and disaster clean up companies** and ask if they do "board ups." They will often board up properties for owners who are leaving their property vacant. Be sure to approach the owner of the company, not the secretary or the workers. The best approach sounds like this, " Mr. Glass Company Owner, how would you like to double your fee on every board up you do?" That question will usually get their attention. Offer to pay the board up company the equivalent of their board up fee when you purchase and profit from the property if they will share those property addresses with you. One more tip on this method, I recommend that you ask the company owner to task his secretary or assistant with sending you a list of each of the board ups they do each week on Friday via email. That way you'll get your list in a timely fashion and have it sent to you regularly without fail. Secretaries are usually more consistent and reliable than company owners.

4. **Hire "bird dogs"** to find vacant and ugly properties for you. Contact people whose job takes them into your focus areas such as newspaper delivery, milk delivery, UPS, FedEx, mailman, lawn care, pest control sprayers, locksmiths, etc. All modern smart phones have a " Geotagging" capability available for use with photographs taken by the phone. Offer to pay them $5 for each digital photo with address of the property tagged to the photo. You could also offer them a much more generous thank you for every property that you end up buying and profiting from,

to the tune of several hundred dollars.

5.   **Put up "bandit" signs** on private property in your focus areas. I currently recommend The Sign Depot in Orlando Florida as a good place to purchase these signs. I want to stress that is important to <u>only</u> put up bandit signs on private property, not public property. Nearly every municipality in North America has enacted ordinances prohibiting placement of commercial signs on public property. That said, very few municipalities have a prohibition on commercial signs placed on private property. Placing signs on public property will, at the very least, get your signs confiscated by the "Sign Police", and at the very worst, result in a hefty fine. What should your sign say? Anything is OK as long as it conveys the message that you buy homes.

6.   **Pass out business cards** to everyone you know and everyone you meet. Sample dialog: "What do I do for a living? I'm a real estate Investor…here's my card." Telling someone that you are a real estate Investor and handing them a card to confirm it, is similar to telling them that you are an astronaut or a rock star or a professional athlete; there is a certain amount of "wow" factor and prestige in telling someone that you're a real estate Investor. I often get the response, "I always wanted to do that, but never had enough time, money, courage, etc., to do it." Also, when you meet someone new, if you tell them about your day job, that typically won't earn you any more money. But if you tell

them you're a real estate Investor, that starts a real estate investment conversation, which could lead to a big payday for you.

7.   **Pass out flyers** indicating you are looking for properties in your focus areas. In Exhibit 20 in the Appendix, there is a sample of the flyer I recommend. Many people are under the mistaken impression that you can only pass out a flier only when you have a property to sell. That's just not true. Passing out a flier letting people know that you're looking for properties can be very effective.

8.   **Send postcards** into your target areas indicating you are looking for properties. Postcards are just miniature versions of your flyer. They're cheaper to print and cheaper to send, and they have the advantage of not needing to be opened like a letter. Nearly everyone reads a postcard, and most people will actually flip it over to read both sides, at least briefly.

9.   **Run classifieds ads** in newspapers and online. In nearly every major city in America, you can use Craigslist ads to find properties. Also, in most markets, there are located online classifieds that in many cases are free. You may ask, " what should my classified ads say?" The truth is, it really doesn't matter what your ad says as long as people know that you're looking for properties. One way to determine appropriate verbiage for an ad is to look at other ads that are being run continuously. If it wasn't working, the creator of the ad would not continue to run it.

10. **Place Magnetic Vehicle Signs or Vehicle Vinyl "Wrap"** on your vehicle. For about $75.00 for a magnetic sign, or $1500 for a vehicle wrap, you can have your message, that you buy homes, driving all over town letting people know what you want and what you do.

11. **Billboards** in lower income areas. Billboards can be expensive but they can also be very effective. If you have the budget for it this could be a great way to get your message out.

12. **Door Hangers**. Door hangers are really just a flier with a hole at the top to go around the doorknob. Hire some neighborhood kids and pay them five or ten bucks to blanket the neighborhood with your door hangers.

13. **Ads on buses, trucks, taxi cabs or other vehicles**. If you have an ad on any kind of commercial vehicle driving around town, that means that your message is also driving around town, all day long. This one thing alone could get you a whole lot of business. If you know someone who owns a business and would allow you to put your ad on their vehicles that could be a gold mine for you. Also, check with the local bus company to see how much a mini billboard on the side of a bus would cost you. Buses have the added benefit of moving continuously, over and over on the same route, thereby giving your message a repetitive nature and, theoretically, making it more effective. Also, it allows your message to be very targeted because you can choose the route over which your message is displayed. You

should only put your bus message on a bus that travels through the areas where you want to find properties.

14. **Bus Benches**. Bus benches are like miniature billboards, only typically, people pay more attention to them than they do big billboards up in the sky. Just like ads on billboards and buses, ads on bus benches can be specifically targeted to areas where you want to find properties.

15. **Direct Mail Letters** into your focus areas using a service such as USPS Every Door Direct Mail, or another professional mailing service.

16. **Google Adwords and/or Adsense and/or Alerts.** If you're familiar with these programs then you already know about them and there's no need for me to discuss them. If you are unfamiliar with the Google Adwords, Adsense, or Alerts programs, you may want to do some research on them. These are programs that allow you to use Google's powerful advertising and search capabilities to help you find properties. Teaching you how to use these programs is way beyond the scope of this book. Simply search on Google for instructions on how to use any of these programs, or find a twentysomething computer nerd that is familiar with them and can help you.

17. **Real Estate Investor's Association or Club.** If you have not yet attended the local real estate Investor clubs, you may want to do that as many people find it very, very helpful. Not only are there resources that can help you find

properties there, but there are many other resources that may be helpful for you and your real estate investment business. If you go to http://www.reiclub.com/ and http://www.creonline.com/ you will find 98% of all the clubs in North America.

18. **Radio Ads.** I'm typically not big into advertising methods where it is difficult to judge the return on money spent. However, I do make an exception when it comes to radio ads. Modern radio advertising is driven by statistics and demographics. In most marketplaces, radio stations generate and analyze statistics regarding their audiences. It is generally possible to be very demographically and geographically targeted with your radio ads. Obviously, you want to focus on demographic groups that are most likely interested in selling their home. For example, people who are retirement age or older often want to sell the family home to either downsize, or move into some kind of assisted living. This of course would present an opportunity for you.

Radio advertising obviously can be quite expensive so I recommend you use this method with caution, and do the best you can to measure the results that you achieve.

19. **Television advertising.** Like radio, television advertising is somewhat demographically and statistically targeted, and may be very effective for you. Also, like radio, it can be very expensive. That said, the proliferation of cable and other types of television programming available may provide you an opportunity to advertise relatively cheaply.

As with radio, and, frankly, any other form of advertising that you pay for, you should always ask your potential customers how they found you, and certainly keep track of that as best you can. If you'll do that you will typically have a better idea of whether not your television or radio advertising dollars are well spent.

20. **Real Estate Agents/MLS.** The National Association of Realtors is the largest trade organization, and one of the best funded and most powerful lobbying groups in North America. Started in 1908, this association has been advertising to the public for more than 100 years. They spent more than $99,000,000 on advertising between 1999 and 2012 alone. The focus of the National Association of Realtors advertising campaign is to create a connection in the brain of the average American. That connection is, " I need to buy or sell a house, therefore, I need to call a real estate agent." "Buy a house, call an agent" has been drummed into our heads for so many years that most Americans believe that is the only way to find a property. I'm not saying that you should avoid using an agent to look for properties. All I'm saying is that if you are counting on your agent to bring you screaming deals, and using them as your exclusive source for finding properties, you're likely to be disappointed. So I include this as a finding method, but please recognize that there are 49 other methods on this list, too. To be a successful Investor, you must overcome the programming you have received from the NAR.

21. **Online Searches**. Wow, there are so many web sites where you can search for properties currently that I don't even know where to begin to tell you to look. You can't even log on your computer without being bombarded by websites advertising properties for sale. A simple Google search will show you more properties than you could ever do something with. That said, please don't think that if you are seeing a property on the Internet, you're the only one in the whole world who is looking at it. Everybody and their brother, and their brothers dog, and the fleas on their brothers dog, knows about that property. Obviously, the more people that know about a property, the more competition there is. The more the competition, the higher the price goes. It is simple supply and demand. I prefer methods of finding properties that are not used by everyone in the world with a personal computing device and an Internet connection. Can you find properties online? Of course you can. All I'm saying is this: Analyze those properties carefully, because they may be overpriced.

22. **Delinquent Property Taxes, Tax Lien or Tax Deed Properties**. I love tax delinquent properties. In most cases they have the two most important factors in negotiating a good deal. Those two factors are equity and urgency. Think about it, if someone is tax delinquent (they didn't pay their taxes when due) it means that their mortgage company didn't collect the taxes and pay them on behalf of the homeowner. Most mortgage companies do this to protect their lien position on the property, since a tax lien moves to

the top of the stack of liens, and trumps any mortgage. Logically then, if someone is tax delinquent, it is likely that they don't have a mortgage on their property. Many tax delinquent properties do have large equity positions. I will tell you from personal experience that it is nearly always easier to negotiate with someone who has a larger rather than smaller equity position in their property. In regards to urgency, every tax lien or tax deed property has a "drop dead" date when either the tax lien owner or the county will foreclose in order to collect unpaid taxes. Yes, a tax delinquent owner can lose their property to foreclosure. This combination of equity and urgency makes for an incredible opportunity for us as Investors.

23. **Property Managers**. Property managers often know when their landlord/owners have a desire to sell their property. You simply contact them and use the "Why your client should work with me" dialogue in Exhibit 5 in the Appendix. What could you do if you had every property manager in your marketplace on the lookout for properties for you?

24. **Free and Clear Property lists**. You can purchase these lists, or, if you have a good relationship with your friendly neighborhood title company, they may provide these lists to you for free! Title companies often have data mining software that will access the county records and search and sort by any number of criteria. They can search by last mortgage origination date and other criteria. If you don't

already have a good relationship with a good title company or title attorney, see Exhibit 7 in the Appendix for an outstanding method to develop that important relationship.

25. **Divorce.** In many cases when two people get divorced they don't want to continue living in the family home. In many cases there are bad memories associated with that property, and they will do anything to avoid that emotional trauma. I certainly sympathize with people's misfortune, and if you think about it, by purchasing their property you're actually helping the divorced people get over their issues and move on with their life. I see myself as helping them, rather than taking advantage.

26. **Pre Foreclosures with Deed Origination dates of 2000 or before.** If someone has been paying on their property for the last 15 years or more, it is likely that they have some kind of an equity position in the property. By targeting pre foreclosures with far back deed origination dates you're increasing the likelihood that you will find someone who has a reasonable equity position in their property.

27. **Foreclosures/REO properties.** In item number 20 on this list I mentioned the "brainwashing" that has been occurring for the last 100+ years perpetrated by the National Association of Realtors. There is another common misconception that has been thrust upon the general public by HUD, Fannie Mae, Freddie Mac and many mortgage lenders in our country. It is the idea that just because a property is a foreclosure, and therefore financially

distressed, it is automatically a great deal. That is just not true. Foreclosures and REO properties can be a good deal, but they are often difficult to wholesale due to the lenders desire to control the transaction. Typically, an REO bank Seller will not accept an assignable contract, for example. Also, because they want to control the title work on the property, they will typically not allow a simultaneous close. That leaves transactional funding as our only exit strategy (with some possible exceptions.) Foreclosures and bank owned properties can work, but may be challenging for the new Wholesaler.

28. **Out of Town/Absentee Owners**. Imagine moving away from your home and then trying to manage it as a rental property from 3000 miles away. Obviously, this could be very challenging and traumatic. As a result, many out of town owners would love to sell their property if you made them an offer. Again, your friendly neighborhood title company or title attorney can often give you a list of these owners from the county records if you ask them for it.

29. **Home Inspectors**. Often, people hire a professional property inspector to inspect their home prior putting it on the market. Sometimes they find out more than they really wanted to know about the condition of their property. In many states if a Seller has a professional property inspection report in hand, they must disclose that information to every potential Buyer of their property. If a property inspector "trashes" their property in the inspection report, many

Sellers get discouraged. If you simply contact them and let them know that you're interested in buying their property, in spite of its terrible condition, you can often put together a deal. What if you had 5, 10, 15 or 20 professional property inspectors who reported to you every time they produced a report on a bad property? Do you think that might help you to find some properties that are in bad condition on which you could make a profit?

30. **Retirement Homes and Assisted Living Centers**. Up to this point but you've probably followed along pretty well with me. But now you're asking yourself "Is this guy crazy? Is he expecting me to go up to that nice little old lady in the nursing home and ask her to sell me her house?" No, that's not what I'm asking you to do it all. But there are two facts that you need to be aware of. Number one, nursing homes are outrageously expensive. According to a recent survey conducted by the Administration on Aging, nursing home rates in America range from a low of $47,000 to $270,000 annually, dependent on where you live. Wow! Number two is the fact is that the vast majority of people who enter assisted living facilities never return to their own home. They are simply incapable of living on their own without assistance. These two facts, combined, present an opportunity for us as real estate Investors. It is very common for the family of the person moving into the assisted living facility to decide to sell that person's home in order to pay for their stay. My suggestion is that you contact the owners or managers of assisted living centers, retirement

centers, and nursing homes. As you can probably imagine, managers and owners of these facilities often struggle to get their big bill paid, and they certainly don't want to throw Grandma out in the snow. If you simply use the script in Exhibit 5, the "why your client should work with me" dialogue, you will find that many facility owners and managers are happy to tell you when one of their tenants needs to sell a home.

31. **Garage Sales**. Often, when people are thinking about moving they hold a garage sale in order to get rid of all their junk. Garage sales can therefore be a good source of finding properties especially if you're already a garage sale aficionado. One of my clients is a garage sale addict. She typically spends all day Friday, Saturday and Sunday visiting garage sales. By simply altering her conversation with the people holding the garage sale, and asking them if they are moving, she has already found three terrific deals.

32. **Utility Workers**. Obviously, if someone is having their power turned off for nonpayment, they're having financial problems. It's possible that those financial problems could at least be partially solved by your purchasing their home. If you know someone who works at a public utility, maybe someone who does billing, or someone who physically goes to a property to turn off the power, etc., that person may be willing to share the addresses of properties where the power has been disconnected, or is scheduled to be disconnected.

33. **Attorneys**. In many cases, when someone is having

problems in their life, they call their attorney. Attorneys are often hired to help solve a variety of legal and financial problems in people's lives. These problems in many cases, may result in the person having a need or desire to sell their house. If, for example, someone decides to get a divorce they will typically discuss the situation with their best friend and their mother. The next person they call is their attorney. If that soon-to-be-ex-spouse meets with their attorney to discuss the divorce, the conversation will always come around to the question, "Do you want to keep the house?" If the soon-to-be-ex-spouse says, "No, I want to sell the house", at that point only the spouses and the attorney know that the house will soon be available for sale. If you have connected with that attorney and let him know that you're interested in buying houses from people in these types of circumstances, they often will counsel with their clients to call you to sell the house. The conversation might go like this, "Susie, I know an Investor who will buy your house. He pays fair prices, he'll give you a written, legitimate offer within 24 hours of seeing your property; he's not an agent so you can avoid paying a commission; you don't have to clean repair or remodel the house because he buys in "as is" condition. He can close quickly, and in many cases he can pay you cash. Here's his number, you should give him a call." Typically, when someone's lawyer tells them to call someone, they do it!

Consider how many divorce attorneys, estate attorneys and probate attorneys there are in your marketplace. These are

56

people who counsel with their clients daily, and many of their clients need to sell a house.

34. **4 "D" Service Providers (Death, Disease, Divorce, Disaster.)** As the saying goes, " Life Happens." At one time or another everyone experiences what I call the 4 D's of life: death, disease, divorce or disaster. These occurrences in people's lives, in many cases, cause them to have a need to sell a house. One person that I taught this concept really internalized it and was excited to start using it. He got out the Sunday newspaper and found all of the obituaries for people who had died the previous week. He reasoned that because these people had died their heirs would want to sell their houses. Believe it or not, his plan was to attend the funerals of these deceased people and pass out his business card to all of the bereaved heirs! Fortunately, I was able to discuss his "brilliant" idea with him before he got to the funerals. Obviously, he would have received a less-than-warm reception from the emotionally distraught relatives and friends. Clearly, the funeral is not the time to talk about the resolution of the dead person's house. The question then begs itself then, "When is the right time to contact the heirs regarding the resolution of the estate?"

Everyone goes through the grieving process at a different rate. So then, how can you tell when the heirs are ready to discuss the sale of the property? The answer is, when they contact someone to help them with it. That someone is what I call a 4 D service provider. In the case of an estate sale, it is typically the estate attorney or the probate attorney. Other 4 D service providers include people who operate nursing homes, assisted living facilities, disaster cleanup companies, insurance companies and anyone else that people might contact to assist them during these difficult times in their lives. That said, attorneys are typically a very good choice to start with, since they serve as a primary 4 D service provider for many people. In the Appendix is a sample of a letter you could write to an estate attorney (Exhibit 8) and you could certainly modify it for any other attorney, or for another type of professional who provides services to people in their times of trouble and need. By the way, the script in Exhibit 5 in the Appendix can be used with any 4 D Service Provider.

35. **Executors/Administrators/Personal Representatives of Estates**. If the deceased person had the knowledge and the means to place their assets in a living trust or some other kind of estate planning entity, there will be an executor or administrator or personal representative who is responsible for the liquidation of the estate's assets. Identifying and contacting these executors can be a great way to find houses. Often, these personal representatives of an estate are noted in the public record or, they will contact the attorney who created the living trust or other estate planning entity, to receive instruction regarding the liquidation of the estate's assets.

36. **Probate**. If the deceased person doesn't place their assets in a living trust or some other entity prior to their

demise, their estate will be probated by the state. Probate is a process by which the state determines how the decedent's assets will be distributed to his or her heirs. By contacting probate attorneys you can often find these estates.

37. **Bail Bondsmen**. Bail bondsmen periodically take houses or other real estate as collateral for a bail bond. When the "suspect" skips bail and heads to South America, the bail bondsman will take the property to satisfy the bond obligation. Unfortunately, the property is often owned by an enabling relative of the accused criminal. When the bail bondsman takes Grandma's free and clear house because "Dear little Johnny" skipped bail, the bail bondsmen is not interested in owning the real estate. As you can imagine, bail bondsmen want money, not real estate. If they know that you are available to buy properties and quickly turn their real property assets into cash they will be willing to contact you. You can use the "why you should work with me" script in Exhibit 6 in the Appendix.

38. **Surplus Properties for Sale**. Cities, counties and states sometimes have surplus properties that they wish to dispose of. Many of these properties are commercial properties but occasionally there are single family homes in the mix. Consider contacting your city, county or state to determine if they have anything available.

39. **Non Profit Organizations (with donated property.)** It is quite common, as part of their tax planning or estate planning efforts, for people donate properties to nonprofit

organizations. In most cases, the nonprofit organization does not want the property, but simply wants the money from it. Simply contact nonprofit organizations in your area using the "why you should work with me" dialog in Exhibit 6 in the Appendix.

40. **Mobile Home Dealers**. Mobile home dealers are the "Grand Central Station" of people moving into and out of home ownership. Often, when people are moving up to homeownership, or down to rentership, they pass through a mobile home. I'm not suggesting that investing in mobile homes is necessarily a good idea, although you may consider it. All I'm saying is, mobile home dealers often know about people in transition.

41. **Process Servers**. In many cases when people are having legal troubles a process is served against. Subpoena or court summonses are examples of documents that are hand delivered to someone, often accompanied by the statement, "You've been served!" Sometimes, this trouble leads them to have a need or desire to sell their house. If you know someone who is a Process Server, they may be able to notify you whenever they serve a legal process on someone, giving you the opportunity to contact that person and offer to buy their house.

42. **Security Guards**. Security guards who patrol housing developments or condo developments are often very friendly and know all the people in the development. If you want a find out what's going on in a condo complex, for

example, find the security guard, bring him some doughnuts, and he'll likely tell you everything you ever wanted to know about the residents of that development. He typically knows who's behind on their homeowners association dues payments, and who's behind on their mortgages, along with who needs to move due to divorce, bankruptcy, foreclosure, job transfer, etc. "Ernie the Security Guard" can be a great person to know, and can provide you with lots of information about the homeowners in that development.

43. **Hard Money Lenders**. As a natural course of their business, sometimes Hard Money Lenders foreclose on properties. As you can imagine, they really don't want the property, they just want to get their money back. If you contact Hard Money Lenders and let them know that you're interested in purchasing any properties that they foreclose on, this could be a great source of properties for you.

44. **Bankers, Mortgage Brokers and other lenders**. There are many ways to use your contacts, connections and friendships with Bankers, Mortgage Brokers and other lenders to your advantage. For example, I know of a mortgage lender who specializes in refinance loans. Any time he turns someone down for a refi, he contacts me with the person's name, address and phone number. I then call them and ask them if they would like to sell their house. Of course, I don't tell them where I got their information. My dialog goes like this, "I noticed your home on Elm Street; I'm

a real estate Investor, I'm buying homes in your area, and I called you today to ask you if you would like to sell your home; do you want to sell?" Note that I didn't say, "I drove by your home on Elm Street" or " Dave at Acme Mortgage told me that he turned you down for refinance loan so I'm calling to take advantage of your misfortune and buy your house." No. no, no! I simply let them believe a that I drove by their house and that is how I came to contact them.

If you think about it logically, there are only two reasons why someone refinances, or attempts to refinance their home. Because they want to lower their payment, or because they need cash out. Just because they were unable to obtain a refinance loan doesn't mean that their need for a lower payment or cash out has disappeared. They still have the need, and selling their house to me may be a good alternative to their refinance.

45. **Private Money Lenders.** Like hard money lenders, private lenders occasionally find it necessary to foreclose on a property. Also, in many cases, private lenders know a lot about properties that are available market place and investment real estate in general.

46. **Homeowner's Associations**. If someone doesn't pay their homeowners association dues, obviously they have financial problems. These financial problems could lead to them having a need or desire to sell their property. If you know or can locate the officers of a homeowners association such as the president, vice president, secretary, or treasurer,

you may be able to find out about people who are behind on their homeowners association dues and approach them about selling their house or condo. Of course, these officers have incentive to alert you to these people because it is in the best interests of the homeowners association for you to purchase the property and resell it to a new Buyer who will actually pay the homeowners association dues. In their eyes, it gives them an opportunity to get rid of a deadbeat.

47. **Tired Landlords**. If you want to have an interesting experience some time, attend eviction court in your marketplace. This is the court where landlords and their tenants go to adjudicate eviction proceedings. You'll never see a more depressed group of landlords in your entire life. In some cases, this experience is the last straw for the owner of a rental property. Simply stand in the back of the courtroom as the burned-out landlord leaves and pass out your business card saying, "If you ever think about selling your property, please call me because I'll buy it."

48. **For Rent Signs and Ads**. When someone puts up a for rent sign or runs a for rent and on a property, they obviously want to rent it out. In some cases, they are burned out, tired landlords, but they just don't know what else to do with the property other than rent it out. Sometimes when you contact them and ask them if they would be willing to sell their answer will be yes.

49. **Insurance Companies (damaged/partially burned houses.)** Insurance companies are often notified when a

home is burned or otherwise damaged. If you know someone, or could create a relationship was someone, who handles insurance claims, they might be willing to share with you the owner's information and the address of the property. In many cases, when a home is damaged, especially by fire, the owner is not intent on repairing the house and back moving in. As you can imagine, a fire in a home can be a traumatic event. Sometimes the homeowner just wants to put those frightening memories behind them and move on to another property, especially if they lost prized possessions, cherished pets or family members in the fire.

50. **Fire Departments (partially burned houses.)** As with the previously mentioned insurance companies, firefighters also, obviously, know about fire damaged or otherwise damaged properties. If you have a friend or relative who is a firefighter, asked them if they will share the addresses of properties where they have extinguished fires, or been called out due to damage, flood, death or other catastrophes.

Some of the above mentioned methods may sound "ghoulish" or feel like you're preying on the misfortune of others. I suggest that you adopt a different perspective. Recognize that in these types of situations, you are offering help and a resolution to someone's problem. I learned long ago that helping people is an important component of your real estate investment business. But don't forget that getting paid to help people is also very important. If you don't get paid to help people, then eventually you may become so financially destitute yourself that you no longer have the financial wherewithal or time to help them. Helping people, and getting paid well to do so is always the best approach.

Step Five

CONTRACTS, CLAUSES, PAPERWORK

As I conduct training sessions with people all over the United States and Canada, I find that one of the biggest fears and concerns that many people have is that of the contracts, otherwise known as the "paperwork." Because for many, this is a new endeavor, they feel very uncertain and anxiuous about which contracts and ancilliary documents are necessary for a real estate transaction to be completed successfully. According to the National Association of Realtors the average American goes through the process of either buying or selling a property somewhere between two and seven times in their entire lifetime. Obviously, because of the infrequency of their exposure to real estate contracts and other documents, they generally are not accustomed to the incredible volume and complexity of the "legalese" verbiage contained in the average state-approved contract. In some states, the standard, state-approved real estate contract can approach 26 pages in length, especially when disclosures, disclaimers and addendums are added. For the uninitiated, these documents can be daunting. I suggest that one way to overcome this anxiety is to do something that many people never even think to do. That is, to actually sit down and read the contract! I'm amazed at how many people actually sign a complex, legally binding real estate contract without fully reading it, and without making a reasonable attempt to understand all of its provisions. From here on out, that person who signs a contract without reading it is not going to be you!

I often say that the real estate Investor who doesn't understand and know how to use the contract is like a carpenter that doesnt know how to use a hammer or a saw. Clearly a carpenter can't do his job without knowledge of how to use his tools. Same goes for you as a real estate Investor. Take the time and make the effort to read the contract and all of the other documents that will likely be part of each of your transactions. It is simply part of becoming a professional and an expert. If you find something in a contract that you don't understand, there is lots of help out there. Your real estate agent, your title company or title attorney, your mortgage lender and others of your team members will often be happy to explain the "legalese mumbo jumbo" of a contract. Also, there is a wealth of information online in blogs, web posts and other places where you can find information about real estate terms, jargon and contract verbiage. Obviously, you want to be careful about not believing everything you read on the Internet, but there is a lot of valid information out there. So, let's get right into "the paperwork".

The Real Estate Purchase Contract

Of course, the first thing we want to discuss is the real estate purchase contract. Throughout this book I'm going to use the term "Real Estate Purchase Contract" but you need to realize that this document goes by different names in different places. Your state's contract, for example, may be called a "Purchase and Sale Agreement" or an "Agreement for the Purchase and Sale of Real Estate" or the "Residential Resale Real Estate Purchase Contract" or "Residential Purchase Agreement and Joint Escrow Instructions" or some other fancy name derived by attorneys who bill by the word. Regardless of what your state calls the standard contract, it is one of our primary tools for purchasing a piece of real estate. That said, I and many others often use a simple, single page, universal purchase contract when working directly with an owner. An example of that single page contract is in the Appendix under Exhibit 9. In the back of the book it appears to be a two page contract, however that is due to the six by nine formatting of the book, and it can easily be printed off on one 8 1/2 by 14 legal size sheet of paper.

It is important that you understand the rules regarding the necessity of the use of the standard state-approved real estate purchase contract. Here is my general rule of thumb: if the property is listed with an agent, a bank owned or REO property, or a short sale property, you must always use the standard, state-approved contract. In most states, it is illegal for a real estate agent to use anything but the standard state-approved contract. Use of anything but the designated contract, constitutes the practice of law which, of course, real estate agents are not allowed to do. Real estate agent's are licensed and allowed to simply fill in the blanks on the standard state-approved boilerplate contract. Some leeway to allow for minor changes is granted them. For example, when they write an addendum to the contract modifying or adding terms. An addendum with minor changes to the main boilerplate provisions of the contract represents the total extent to which an agent can be "creative" in a contract, according to the law.

The other two instances in which you must use a standard state-approved contract are when a bank or lender is directly involved in the decision-making process of the sale of the property. A bank-owned property, and a short sale property, because they require approval of a lender, should always be put on the standard state-approved contract. The lenders are very much "in-the-box" thinkers. They have a certain paradigm regarding how a real estate transaction should be conducted. In their way of thinking, only the standard state-approved contract represents a legitimate agreement. Anything else, from their perspective, represents a riskier transaction. The last thing the lender wants is to deal with someone who has submitted a contract that they got from a late night infomercial, get rich quick real estate guru. In regards to a bank owned property or a short sale property, the lender always views themselves as the victim. From their perspective, they loaned the money in good faith, and the "evil Borrower" didn't keep their end of the agreement. Their viewpoint is best summarized by the old expression, "Cheat me once, shame on you; cheat me twice, shame on me." They always feel as though they have been cheated and therefore, will only accept what they think of as a "normal" contract. If you submit anything but the standard state-approved contract to an REO lender-owner (or to a lender in a short sale transaction) they will simply roll your offer up in a ball and throw it away.

All of that said, if there is not a real estate agent or a lender-owner involved in the transaction, anything other than the standard state-approved contract can be used. Theoretically, you could sit down with the Seller at Denny's and write out the terms of your agreement on a gravy-stained napkin. As long as both parties sign the agreement, whatever was written on the napkin becomes legal and binding. That said, I don't recommend that you do this. As already mentioned, I recommend you use a simple form of an agreement such as the one in Exhibit 9 in the Appendix.

If you think about it, approaching an inexperienced, unsophisticated, anxious Seller with a multipage, "legalese mumbo jumbo" filled contract can be intimidating to that Seller. In my experience, it is much easier to get them to sign the simple, one page contract. After all, it only contains nine provisions and the verbiage of those nine provisions is normal, understandable English. Also, if you notice, there's a lot of white space on this contract. Again, the purpose of using this contract is to reduce the Seller's anxiety.

Of course, a more relaxed Seller is more likely to say "Yes" and sign the contract. In my experience, if you present most Sellers with the standard real estate purchase contract, their knee-jerk response will be to consult with their brother in law, who is a real estate agent, or their uncle, who is an attorney. Most of the time, when you involve a real estate agent or an attorney in this type of transaction, your deal will blow up. The unsophisticated, anxious Seller will be advised by their real estate agent or attorney not to sell you the property, or at least, to ask you for a higher price. Obviously, this can be disastrous for you. By using the simple, one page contract, you can, in most cases, avoid the often negative intervention of an agent or attorney. I strongly recommend that you use a simple one page contract or something like it when working with an unrepresented Seller.

Other Contract Considerations

Regardless of whether you use the standard state-approved contract or something else, it is very important that you add some clauses to what ever contract you end up using. As I mentioned, the contracts, forms and documents are often a great source of anxiety to a new wholesale Investor.

One of the main reasons new Investors hesitate and are reluctant to place an offer on a property is because they are concerned that there will be some unrecoverable, catastrophic financial consequences of their real estate contract dealings. If this describes you, sit down, relax, take a deep breath, and stop worrying. If you will simply see to it that the wholesaling clauses included in Exhibit 10 are included in all of your contracts, whether those created by a real estate agent, or some other contract you use, the chances of you making a catastrophic, unrecoverable financial mistake in your real estate contract will be negligible. Those clauses, combined with minimized earnest money deposits, will reduce your risk in any deal to the amount of earnest money you have given the Seller, period.

When first reading these clauses, some people are concerned about the nature of number six. Clause number six states, "In the event that the Buyer defaults or does not perform on any provision of this agreement for any reason, the Seller shall retain the earnest money deposit as their sole remedy under this agreement." Sometimes when I share this clause with people they say to me, "but Tim, I don't wanna give up my earnest money deposit!" Well, neither do I. But you must understand that the potential for loss in most states is much greater than just your earnest money deposit. Compared to the other two avenues of recourse that a Seller likely has in your state, losing your earnest money is a very desirable outcome.

In nearly every state, if the Buyer defaults, or, in layman's terms, doesn't do what they said that they would do in the contract, the Seller has two other forms of recourse available to them, in order to be "made whole" as the attorneys call it. Both can be extremely nasty and undesirable.

The first avenue of "recourse" that the Seller may have is a lawsuit for "Specific Performance." Specific performance means taking you to court to enforce the contract, thereby forcing you to purchase the property. Obviously, this could be disastrous for you. If for any reason you have decided not to purchase this property and you default, the court forcing you to purchase would not be a desirable outcome for you. The court could easily require you to:

 1) Accept a loan that is unacceptable to you, or

 2) Use your own personal funds to purchase the property, or

3) Force you to liquidate your assets in order to come up with the money to close on the property and perform on the contract.

Clearly, none of these outcomes would be good.

While a lawsuit for specific performance is not good, the second avenue of "recourse" for the Seller is even worse for you. If the Seller can prove to the court that he was financially damaged by the fact that you didn't close on the property, he can get a judgment against you for the amount of those "actual and compensatory" damages. Typically, damages are easy to establish in court. If, for example, someone came to the Seller after he had the property under contract with you and said, " Mr. Seller, I want to buy your house and I'll pay you X dollars for it", the testimony of that Buyer and the amount that they were willing to pay for the property could establish a dollar amount by which the Seller was financially damaged because you didn't close. Damage awards of $10,000, $20,000, $50,000, or $100,000 are not uncommon. Wow!

I don't know about you, but to me risk of a specific performance lawsuit, or a lawsuit for damages is never ever, ever, ever an acceptable risk. In fact, my personal business policy is to never sign a contract that does not include clause number six, period. The risk is just too great. I strongly suggest that you adopt the same policy for your real estate investment business.

Occasionally, you will receive some resistance to some of the clauses. For example clause number two would theoretically allow you to do anything you wanted regarding the marketing of the property. You could, if you desire to do so, place a 30 foot tall, inflatable guerrilla (like the ones you see down at the car dealer on Saturday) on the front lawn of the property! (By the way, I do not suggest you do this!) Usually, the assurance that you aren't going to do anything outrageous in regards to marketing their property is enough to reduce the concerns of the Seller regarding this clause.

From time to time, you will run into a Seller that doesn't want you to put a sign in front of their property. It typically means that they don't want the neighbors to know that they're moving. Usually, when they tell me they don't want me to put a sign in front of the property, I ask them if they'd mind if their neighbors thought they were selling drugs? Of course, they always say "no, what do you mean?" I simply explain to them that showing a property and doing a drug deal looks the same from the neighbors point of view. A fancy car drives up to the property, people get out, they go inside the house for about 5 minutes, they come back out, get back into the car, and drive away. Ask any police officer or DEA agent and they will tell you that that is the perfect description of how a drug deal happens. I say this in jest of course, but I have used this line on a Seller to encourage them to allow me to place a sign in front of their property, and it does work.

Clause number three sometimes causes anxiety on the part of the Seller. If the property is unoccupied, it's usually not a problem. The trouble arises when the property is occupied, especially by an owner's tenant, or by the owner himself. He states that he doesn't want you walking in on his wife while she is in the shower at 7:00 AM or 7:00 PM. To eliminate the Sellers concern, simply negotiate a time frame for notice of your viewing of the property. For example, you could say, "Showing with two hours notice, or, 4 hours notice." This type of agreement for notice will typically eliminate the Sellers concerns about this clause.

Depending upon what you put as the number of days in

clause number four, you may receive some resistance. Usually I put 21 days in that clause, and sometimes Sellers don't like that. If they object, I tell them, "My property inspector is not on my payroll; he is an independent contractor with his own business. I can't control his availability or his hours, and he's a very busy guy. You have my assurance that I will do everything I can to get the inspection done sooner than 21 days, but I'm just putting you on notice that it may take up to 21 days to get the job done." This response usually eliminates the Seller's concerns.

The other thing that I should mention at this point is my recommendation for the number of days you build into your contract for the closing deadline. I typically ask for 45 days from the date that I'm writing the contract or from the date of the acceptance of the contract by the Seller. I do this in order to allow plenty of time for me to find a Buyer for my property. You will from time to time get some objections on this " far out" closing deadline. If the Seller objects to my long closing date I tell him the truth, and simply say, "Mr. Seller, yours isn't the only deal on working on. Also, notice the way it's worded with the closing date as a deadline. As it says here in the contract, we will close on *or before* the date that I have indicated. Mr. Seller would you be offended if I called you in a few days or a week and told you that I was ready to close?" Invariably they say that that would be ideal for him. I then say, "Obviously, that would be ideal for me too, because then I will make my money that much sooner on the property. You have my assurance that I will close this as soon as I can but, I want you to know that I may need up to 45 days to close." Usually, this removes the objection to the 45 day closing date. If not, consider a shorter period of time, but make sure that you allow yourself enough time to find a Buyer. The last thing that you want is to go through all the trouble finding the Seller, putting it under contract and then not having enough time to find a Buyer and defaulting on the contract as a result.

Other 'Paperwork'

The purchase contract is an important document that you will need to learn about and use. But it is certainly not the only thing that you'll need. We will now discuss the other important documents you'll need for your wholesale real estate transactions.

Assignment of contract form

Depending upon which exit strategy you use (see chapter one, "Understanding the Basics of Wholesaling") you may need an assignment of contract form. I have included an example of one in Exhibit 11 in the Appendix. If you don't like this one, they are all over the Internet; simply go out and find one you like.

Filling out this form is self-explanatory, but keep in mind the roles that each of the parties are playing in this agreement. Remember, this agreement is taking the place of a real estate purchase contract between you and the Buyer. Technically, you are not selling the property to the Buyer, because, frankly, you don't own it yet; all you really own is the right to purchase the property. With an assignment of contract exit strategy you are not selling the property, but rather, are selling your contractual right to purchase the property; you are selling the contract itself.

What if the Buyer changes his mind?

I am often asked the question, "What do I do if the Buyer changes his mind and decides not to buy my property?" This is often a great source of anxiety for new Wholesale Investors. I suggest that one of the best things you can do to keep your Buyer motivated and committed to your transaction is to ask for a large, non-refundable, upfront earnest money deposit either in the assignment of contract form, or in the purchase agreement that you create between you and the Buyer. A large non-refundable earnest money deposit forces the Buyer to either perform, or forfeit said large deposit. Either way, you win. In a perfect world, the Buyer would pay you your entire assignment fee as a non-refundable deposit. Sometimes, however, you will run into a Buyer who is not comfortable in giving you your entire assignment fee up front. You can do whatever you want for your business, but my personal business policy is to insist upon ½ of my total wholesale fee upfront as a non-refundable deposit. That way, if everything goes to "heck in a handbasket" and the Buyer backs out, I still have profited from the deal.

If the Buyer does decide to back out at the last minute, and forfeit his earnest money deposit, you can often use some of that money to encourage the Seller to extend the deadline of the contract several weeks or longer. This could allow you to use that extra time to find another Buyer for the property. It is typically much easier to convince a Seller to extend your closing deadline if you offer him an additional, non-refundable earnest money deposit. If, for example, you were to get a $5000 upfront non-refundable earnest money deposit from your Buyer and he were to default and forfeit his deposit, you could offer your Seller $1000 or $2000 to extend the contract for 2 to 4 weeks. Even if you gave him $2000, and everything fell apart, you still would have made $3000 from that transaction. Not as good as $10,000 or $5000, but better than a poke in the eye with a sharp stick, as they say.

What if the Seller changes his mind?

Another logical question considers what to do if the Seller changes his mind and decides not to sell you the property. There is a special document that we can use to keep the Seller from selling the property to someone else, thereby cutting us out of the deal. It is called an Affidavit and Memorandum of Agreement Concerning Real Estate. There is an example of one in Exhibit 12 in the Appendix. It is simply a public records notification of the fact that you and the Seller have a contract together. That said it does not require the Seller's OK, approval, or even his knowledge of its existence. It is filed with the county recorder's office, and becomes part of the public record. It is not a lien, a mortgage or any other kind of encumbrance against the property. It is, considered a "cloud" on the title. A "cloud" is an item of question in regards to the title of the property. Once it has been filed, the person who filed it is the only one who can remove it from the public records. Until the cloud is removed, no title company on the earth will close that deal. Why you ask? Because title companies and title attorneys provide title insurance on real estate transactions. That title insurance policy covers any misktakes or unknown issues on the title. Obviously then, a cloud on the title raises their liability. If the Buyer sues the Seller for defaulting on the contract and selling the property to someone else, and the Buyer wins the lawsuit, typically the title insurance company's title policy will cover the Sellers obligation to the Buyer to provide a free and clear title. Title insurance companies, just like any other insurance company, have an ideal business model; take in lots and lots of premiums, all without ever paying out any claims. Because of this fact the title insurance company will not close a deal with any unresolved "clouds" on the title.

Imagine, for example, that I make an offer on a property at $100,000. Sam Seller signs my contract accepting my offer, and now we both anticipate the closing coming up in 45 days. The next day however the Seller receives an offer from another Buyer, let's call him Bob Buyer, for $120,000, $20,000 more than my offer. An honest Seller will tell Bob that he is already committed to sell me the property. A dishonest Seller though, may think to himself, "Bob is offering me $20,000 more than Tim. I want to take Bob's offer not Tim's offer!" He then accepts Bob's offer, ignoring the fact that he already has an accepted offer with me. Once the offer is signed by both Bob and Sam, Sam will send that offer to his friendly neighborhood title company or title attorney to begin the title search. Of course the title company will find my cloud on Sam's title. When they do, they will contact Sam, will tell him about my Affidavit and Memorandum of Agreement Concerning Real Estate, and will further tell him that he must have it removed a prior to them closing the deal, otherwise they will not close it. I then get a call from Sam and the conversation goes as follows:

Sam: "Hey Tim, this is Sam."

Tim: "Hi Sam how are you. I'm looking forward to our closing."

Sam: "Yeah Tim, that's what I'm calling you about. I've decided to sell the house to someone else.

Tim: "Oh, I'm sorry to hear that Sam...but I guess that's your choice."

Sam: "Well, that's the reason I'm calling. I got a call from my title company and they told me that you filed some "affidavit thingy" against my property."

Tim: "Yes I did Sam."

Sam: "Well, it seems that my title company won't close the transaction with my new Buyer until you remove your affidavit from the public records. So I'm calling you to ask you to remove that for me."

Tim: "Gee Sam, I'm happy to do that for you, for the measly sum of $10,000. Bring me a cashier's check for it today and I will have it removed from the record tomorrow."

You get the idea. This document prevents the Seller from going around you. Some people ask me if I use this on every property. The answer is no, not necessarily. But if you have any inkling at all that the Seller may try to go around you, spend the money on the fee to file it because it will be very cheap insurance against the Seller backpedaling on you. I don't know how much it costs where you live, but in my market its $12.00 to file it with the county recorder's office. What a bargain.

By the way, the county recorder's office may call it something else where you live. If they don't recognize the term, "Affidavit and Memorandum of Agreement Concerning Real Estate" then simply show them a copy of the agreement that I have given you and ask them what the equivalent for your marketplace is called.

The end of the 'paper trail'

In order to be more complete and conscientious, I have included three additional forms in the Appendix. Exhibit 13 is a Contract to Sell Real Estate. This form can be used when you have a Buyer who wants to buy your property, but does not have a contract of his own. Please read it carefully, and *don't use it when buying a property, only when selling the property.* If you read it carefully, you will notice that particular contract is somewhat slanted to the advantage of the Seller, not the Buyer. That is why I suggest you use it to sell rather than to buy.

Next, in Exhibit 14, is a generic addendum for a contract. If, after you and the Seller have agreed to the simple, one page contract, as in Exhibit 9, you need to make changes to your agreement, this is the type of addendum you may want to use.

Finally, from time to time unfortunately, it will be necessary for you to cancel a contract. In Exhibit 15 I have included an example of a cancellation letter that you might use in order to cancel a contract with the Seller.

FINDING BUYERS FOR YOUR PROPERTIES

Some real estate investment trainers will tell you that you must go out and find Buyers for your properties *before* you start to look for properties. They will tell you that your Buyers list is a critical piece of your real estate investment business. I agree that it is a critical piece, but I strongly disagree that finding Buyers prior to finding properties is critical. In the current market in North America, our biggest challenge is finding Sellers who will sell their property at a price that fits into our formula. Once you find a property that fits into the formula, selling it is relatively easy. As I mentioned before, there are more Investors in the marketplace now than there have ever been, and they are all hungry to find good properties. If you place a property under contract at a price that will appeal to your Fix & Flip Investor Buyers, and then advertise it minimally, they will hunt you down like a fugitive. That is the reason I have saved the discussion of finding Buyers until the end. It's just not that hard these days.

Wholesale Buyer Finding

I will now share with you nine different ways to find Buyers for your wholesale properties. Understand, these are not the only ways to find Buyers they are just the methods that I think are the most effective. My suggestion is that when you have a wholesale property under contract, you should implement each of the methods on the list until you either sell the house, or have implemented all the methods, whichever comes first.

Finding a Wholesale Buyer

1) Call all of the "We Buy Homes" signs and websites for your area

Sometimes when I recommend that someone call all of the 'we buy homes' signs and web sites for their area (sometimes known as bandit signs) people say to me, "Gee Tim, aren't I just calling my competition?" My answer is, you may be, but there are a lot of Fix & Flip Investors and Buy & Hold Investors that use bandit signs to attract Sellers. I personally have trained thousands of Fix & Flip Investors to post those signs, and so have many other trainers. Just because someone posts a bandit sign, don't assume that they are a Wholesaler.

When you call one of the signs or websites, simply ask them, "What kind of Investor are you; are you a Fix & Flip Investor, a Buy & Hold Investor, or a Wholesaler?" Any time I meet another Investor, regardless of the venue, I always ask that question. Ask them what they like to do and let them tell you. Yes, you will find some other Wholesalers. But you'll also find some Fix & Flip Investors and some Buy

& Hold Investors who are very interested in your property.

2) Run an ad in the local paper and online classifieds for your area

Below is an example of the type of ad you might run. Truth be told, it really doesn't matter what your ad says, as long as you let people know that your property is available and that it's a good deal.

INVESTOR SPECIAL-- NEEDS WORK!

3 bedroom, 2 bath brick house

After repair value $200,000;
Repairs $30,000; Asking price
$110,000 cash O.B.O

Wow, what a bargain!

Call 801– 555– 1212

---

3) Make and distribute a flyer about your property to all the local real estate investment clubs

Make up a flyer like the one in Exhibit 16 in the Appendix and circulate it to all the members of all the real estate investment clubs in your marketplace. If you haven't yet identified the local real estate investment clubs in your area, now would be a great time to do that. Here are the two websites I recommend where you will find 97% of all the real estate investment clubs in North America:

http://www.reiclub.com/real-estate-clubs.php

http://www.creonline.com/Real-Estate-Investment-Clubs/index.html

http://www.meetup.com/

Many real estate investment clubs only meet once a month. If you put the property under contract a day or two after the last meeting, you will have to wait nearly a month to contact all of the Investors there and pass out a flier. Obviously that's not going to work. I suggest that you contact the president, owner or operator of the various local real estate investment clubs as soon as you get a new property under contract. (You did make it a point to introduce yourself to the president of the club at the last meeting, didn't you? If not, shame on you!)

Simply call them and ask them if they have the e-mail addresses of all the club members. They typically do. Tell them you have a hot new property and that, being a loyal club member, you wanted to notify the club members first before advertising it to the general public. Ask them if they will forward a copy of your flyer to all the club members as soon as possible. Generally speaking, they are very happy to do so.

4) Put a hand-lettered or professionally printed sign in the yard, preferably neon green or neon orange

According to the National Association of Realtors a yard sign contributes significantly to the sale of a property about 70% of the time. We don't want to miss out on that benefit. Your yard sign could simply be a repeat of the classified ad shown above, or whatever else you want to do.

5) Go to the foreclosure auction and meet other Investors there

This is my favorite method of finding Buyers for wholesale properties. Let me tell you how it works.

You simply attend the foreclosure auction in your market. Exhibit 17 in the Appendix will help you to locate your local foreclosure auction. Auctions are free, and open to the public. There are no tickets or admission or reservations or anything like that; you just show up at the appropriate time and you can stand there and watch. In many instances they are held on the courthouse steps, the lobby of the courthouse building or some other public venue. Please understand, I am *not* suggesting that you go bid on properties at the auction. I'm simply suggesting that you go to the auction to meet other Investors there.

I don't know what the terms are for the foreclosure auction in your marketplace, but let me tell you what it's like in my marketplace. Anyone that wants to watch can watch. But if someone wants to bid on properties and purchase a property at the auction, that's a different story. In order to bid on properties you must bring in a $5000 cashier's check written out to the auctioneer. You also sign registration papers with your name and other pertinent information. Additionally, you sign an agreement indicating that if yours is the successful bid on a particular property, your $5000 earnest money deposit becomes non-refundable. Further, you agree in writing that if you are the successful bidder, you will bring in the balance owed in the form of another cashier's check within 24 hours of your successful bid.

In the history of the world, there has never been a new mortgage generated within 24 hours. Mortgages simply take a lot longer than that to happen. As a consequence of this fact we know two important things about every single person standing there at the foreclosure auction bidding on properties:

1) **They are interested in purchasing discounted properties, otherwise they wouldn't be there.**

2) The have CASH!

If there are any other qualifications to describe the perfect Buyer for my wholesale properties, I don't know what they are.

When you meet them there, here is the conversation I suggest you have with them after you have introduced yourself to them:

You: "Do you only buy properties at the foreclosure auction, or would you consider buying a property from another source that represents a good buy?"

Them: "Yes, I would consider anything; what do you have?"

If you have a property under contract simply reach in your briefcase, pull out a flier (like the one in Exhibit 16) and hand it to them.

If you don't have a property under contract at the time, you simply say, "I'm between properties right now, but I anticipate in the next week or two I will have another one. Would you like me to call you?" They will invariably respond with an emphatic "Yes!"

6) **Contact remodeling contractors to ask if they buy properties to rehab**

Sometimes the owners of remodeling contractor companies purchase properties to fix and flip. It makes sense, since they typically have access to cheap labor and cheap materials. You simply talk with the owners of rehab and remodeling companies and asked them if they buy properties for rehab. A little tip, don't ask the secretary or the receptionist or the workers that are on the site; find the owner and ask him.

7) **Contact all the obvious "Investor" owners**

Contact all the obvious Investor owners in the same area as your property by looking up the street in the county records and ask if they would like to buy another property in that area. Most county records allow you to search by different data fields. If you can search by street name, you will get a list of all of the owners on a particular street, and adjacent streets if you search for that. In many cases you will see that the owners of record are obvious owner occupants. When you see names like Tabitha and Kevin Bailey, Robert and Susan Smith, Bruce and Karen Hardwick, and Jedediah Brown, you know those folks are owner occupants. When you see names like High Tide Investments LLC, Wind River Investments LTD., or McNabb Property Enterprises Inc., you know those folks are Investors. Simply call him up and say, "I noticed your property at 142 Elm Street. Since you already have a property in that neighborhood I'm calling to ask if you would like to buy another one because I have one for sale at 153 Elm Street. Do you want to buy another rental property in that area?" In many cases you will find that they do indeed want to buy another rental property in that area. There are economies of scale and convenience that can make having multiple properties in one area very desirable. If all of your properties are in one area it makes it much easier to collect rents, do maintenance and repairs, show properties, and do property inspections. These landlords may just want to purchase your property.

Sometimes when making these calls you will find that a landlord owner is less than enthusiastic about the ownership of his current property. He may say things like, "I really don't want to buy another property in that neighborhood; in fact, I don't like the property I have there. My tenants are always causing trouble, there is lots of crime and graffiti in the area, and I have a difficult time collecting rents and maintaining my property. I don't want to buy another property in that area because I don't even like the one I have there!" In this instance, you didn't just find a Buyer for your property, you found a Seller! Simply say to him, "In addition to selling properties in the area, we are also buying properties in the area. Would you consider selling your property?" Then use the Seller Script (Exhibit 2) to figure out whether not you want to buy that property.

8) **Call "For Rent" ads**

Call "For Rent" ads in your area and say, "I saw your 'For Rent' ad. Since you already own a rental property in this area, do you want to buy another one?" You would you then use the same script as shown above.

9) **Ask your title company** for some help

Having a relationship with a title company or title attorney is like having the key to the information vault regarding properties in your marketplace. Ask your title company to do a public records search of properties whose owners paid cash and are non-owner occupied (physical address of property is different than the owner's mailing address for tax notices.) Contact those owners and ask if they would like to buy another income producing property.

Certainly, these are just some of the methods that you can use to find Buyers, and there are many others. The point that I'm trying to make here is that finding properties is typically a bigger challenge than finding Buyers. If you will simply use the 50 ways to find properties and go out and find some properties that fit into the formula, Buyers will beat a path to your door.

Step Seven

PUTTING IT ALL TOGETHER, STEP BY STEP

To briefly recap, in chapter one we went over the basics of wholesaling. In chapter two I showed you how identify your focus neighborhoods where you will focus your finding efforts. In chapter three we went over 50 different ways to find properties. Chapter four was all about analyzing properties and figuring out whether not a particular property was a good deal for your wholesale property Buyer, and therefore for you as a Wholesaler. In chapter five be talked about the paperwork and the various different forms with which you need to become familiar. Chapter six of course was all about finding Buyers for your wholesale properties. Now, in chapter seven were going to put it all together.

As I mentioned in the beginning I take a step by step, checklist approach to wholesaling real estate. Below is a checklist that you can follow that will asure your success as a wholesale real estate Investor. If you will persistently and relentlessly follow these steps you cannot fail. Remember, by definition, the only time you fail is if you stop and give up trying. Persistence, determination and an orientation towards action are the three major characteristics of successful 21st century real estate Investors. Massive action solves all problems. It is not easy, but it is simple. If you will commit to take massive action in finding properties, recognizing that, to a large degree it is a numbers game, you will be successful, period. Please realize that you will need to make offers on somewhere between 25 to 100 properties before you will have one successful deal close. That's just the way it is. You certainly could have success sooner than that, but if you haven't made at least 100 written offers on properties you haven't yet done enough work. If you don't get a property within your first 100 offers, persist and you will get one in your second 100 offers. Les Brown, a renowned motivational speaker, is very famous for saying, "It's not over until I win!" If you adopt his attitude and never give up, you will win. Maybe not today, maybe not this week or this month, but eventually you will win. Failure is simply giving up and stopping before you reach your success.

Wholesale Flight Plan Checklist

☐ **Set up your business (minimally)**

    o Business Cards

    o Phone

o Bandit Signs

o Access to County Records (netronline.com)

o Relationship with real estate agent who is willing to share MLS info

o Relationship with a title company or title attorney

o Business Plan (use the template in Exhibit 19 in the Appendix)

☐ **Identify your focus neighborhoods**

o Neighborhoods that are at or below the Median Price for Single Family homes in your area. Affordable neighborhoods with modest houses in Low to Middle income areas

o Neighborhoods that are predominantly 3 Bedroom, 2 Bath Homes

o Low <u>Days On Market</u> neighborhoods (30 to 60 to 90 days maximum)

o Within a 30 minute driving radius of where you live or work or where you spend a lot of your time

- You can ask your agent for advice and help or figure out your areas on Trulia.com or a combination of both of these methods.

☐ **Begin to market for properties**

- Immediately implement the first 7 marketing methods from Chapter Three plus your choice of 3 to 20 others

- Join as many local real estate investment clubs as are available in your marketplace

- Pass out your business cards to everyone you know and everyone you meet

☐ **Analyze all properties you find**

- Research and find the accurate After Repair Value

- Estimate repairs

- Use the formula in the chapter one to figure out the correct Maximum Purchase Price for your Investor Buyer

- Subtract your desired wholesale fee from your Investor Buyer's Maximum Purchase Price to calculate your offer price to Seller o Make the offer at your offer price

☐ **Focus on making offers, not negotiating/analyzing**

    o Remember, close counts in horseshoes, hand grenades and wholesaling. When in doubt, make an offer, get the property under contract and shop it to the marketplace; if you're wrong, the market will quickly tell you so

    o Make lots and lots of offers! Remember, nothing happens in your business until you make an offer.

☐ **Put a property under contract with a Seller**

    o Use Standard State-Approved Real Estate Purchase Contract when an agent is involved

    o Use Short Form Real Estate Purchase Contract when no agent is involved

☐ **Find a Buyer for your Under Contract property**

    o Immediately implement all methods in chapter six on finding a wholesale Buyer. Continue to implement these methods until you either sell

your property or have implemented
everything on the list, whichever comes first

☐ **Put a property under contract with a Buyer**

- o Use the following forms as appropriate:

    - ▪ Assignment of Contract form or

    - ▪ Standard State-Approved Real Estate Purchase Contract or

    - ▪ Short Form Real Estate Purchase Contract

☐ **Exit the deal as appropriate**

- o Assignment of Contract to Buyer or

- o Simultaneous Closing or

- o Transactional Funding

☐ **Repeat steps 3 through 9 above**

- o Do it again, and again, and again, and again until you reach your income goals.

As I said before, it is not easy, but it is simple. If you will diligently follow and accomplish steps one through ten you will be successful; it is inevitable.

Persistence is Everything!

Persistence is the number one most important personal characteristic of a successful 21st century real estate Investor. If you will persist through every obstacle and challenge, you *will* win.

Michael Jordan, arguably the most famous and successful basketball player of all time, has been quoted as saying:

"I've missed more than 9000 shots in my career. I've lost almost 300 games. 26 times, I've been trusted to take the game winning shot and missed. I've failed over and over and over again in my life. And that is why I succeed."

You *will* run into challenges and obstacles in your real estate Investment business…it is inevitable. If you will simply continue and persist through the failures, you will not ultimately fail but will succeed. Failure is simply quitting before you succeed. If you don't quit, by definition, you can't fail.

Calvin Coolidge, a Republican attorney from Vermont, a small-government conservative and the 30th President of the United States, who was born on the 4th of July, clarified it for us almost 100 years ago:

"Nothing in the world can take the place of Persistence.

Talent will not; nothing is more common than unsuccessful men with talent.

Genius will not; unrewarded genius is almost a proverb.

Education will not; the world is full of educated derelicts.

Persistence and Determination alone are omnipotent.

The slogan 'Press On' has solved and always will solve the problems of the human race."

Incredibly, we are now more than 16 years into the 21st century! It's about time real estate Investors finally come into the new century with practical, current, leading edge investment methods critical to their success today. That's what this book is all about. That, and persistence. As I said before, persistence is the most important characteristic necessary to become a successful real estate Investor in the new economy and the new century.

You now have everything you need to become a successful wholesale real estate Investor. The only ingredient missing now is your effort and consistency in following the steps outlined above. I urge you to take action today, and I wish you all the best.

Tim Bell

http://www.wholesaleflightplan.com/

Appendix

Exhibit 1--Seller Letter

Dear Property Owner,

I am a local real estate Investor buying properties in your neighborhood. My partners and I buy properties, fix them up as needed and resell them to nice families, making the neighborhood a better place to live for everyone! I noticed your vacant property on Elm St. and I am interested in buying it.

If you are interested in selling or know someone who is please contact my office at 801-555-1212

- ✓ **I pay fair prices**

- ✓ **I will give you a legitimate, written offer within 24 hours of viewing your property**

- ✓ **I'm not a real estate agent, so you can save a 6% or 7% commission by selling to me instead of listing with an agent**

- ✓ **You don't need to clean, repair, remodel or even clear out the property because I buy in "as is" condition**

- ✓ **You don't need to waste time marketing and showing your property, running the risk of listing it with an agent and not having it sell because I'll buy it right now!**

- ✓ **I can act quickly…you tell me when you want to close**

Call me now…I can help you!

Tim Bell, Principle Property Buyer, Property Partners 801-555-1212

Check us out online at propertypartners.com

Exhibit 2--Seller Script

This dialog allows you to obtain the information you need to make a quick assessment of any property to determine if it will fit into your formula.

PHONE CALL: *"Hello, my name is _____ I'm a local real estate Investor, I'm buying properties in the area. I noticed your property on _____ Street and I'm calling to ask you if you want to sell your house...do you want to sell it?"*

IN PERSON: *"Hello, my name is _____ I'm a local real estate Investor, I'm buying properties in the area. I stopped by today to ask you if you want to sell your house...do you want to sell it?"*

YES or Maybe

"Tell me about the property"

Number of Bedrooms? ____

Number of Bathrooms? ____

Square Footage (approximate is OK if they are unsure)? _____

Lot Size (approximate is OK if they are unsure)? _____

Year Built (approximate is OK if they are unsure)? _____

Garage/Carport? _____

Exact Address (if you don't already have it) _____

What is the condition of the property?

_____

_____

"How much is it WORTH?" _____

How much do you OWE on it?" _____

"How much do you WANT for it?" _____

"Great, let me check the records on your property, do some research and I'll get back to you with an offer. What is the best number to call you on during the day?"

NO

"Could you please help me to understand what you have in mind... Your property is obviously run down and vacant (if it is)... Why you don't want to sell it?"

Regardless of what they say, you say, "So you are sure that you don't want to sell?"

"I understand. Here is my card in case you change your mind. Will you call me if things change?"

Give them your name and phone number, or your business card if you are there in person.

Follow up with them once a month via phone or mail:

"I'm just calling to see if your circumstances have changed and you've decided to take my offer on your house...would you sell it to me now?"

Finally, put them on a mailing list and mail to them once a month offering to buy their house

Exhibit 3--General or Miscellaneous Costs

Closing, Holding, Carrying and Sales Costs
(Also known as General Costs or Miscellaneous Costs, typically 10% or so of ARV)

Closing Costs To Buy
o   Title, Escrow, Closing and Attorney's Fees
o   Transfer Taxes
o   Lender Fees, Loan Points, Appraisal
o   Recording, Doc Prep and other miscellaneous title company charges
o   Up front points or other up front loan costs

Holding Costs
o   Utilities
o   Insurance- Hazard and Liability
o   Supplies
o   Taxes
o   Mortgage Payments

Closing Costs To Sell
o   Title, Escrow, Closing and Attorney's Fees
o   Transfer Taxes
o   Commissions
o   Buyer Concessions
o   Recording, Document Preparation and other   miscellaneous title company charges
o   Interest, points, etc. on the money you borrowed to put the deal together

The above list represents some typical costs generally associated with buying, holding and selling a property, but there may be others in your area. Be sure to research these costs thoroughly for your market before you buy or sell. The easiest way to do this is by checking with your local team members (real estate agent, title company, real estate attorney, mortgage loan officer, insurance agent, etc.) Be sure to get accurate estimates of these "costs" as they can vary widely from market to market. In some markets and under some loan terms, the "10%" portion of the "70% rule" may not be enough to cover those costs. Please check before you buy.

The easiest way to clearly determine these costs is to have your title company prepare a **"Proposed, Estimated or Pro Forma HUD Closing Disclosure Statement** (formerly known as the HUD-1 Settlement Statement)." This is a document which shows all the charges involved in a real estate transaction and appropriately distributes the monies involved in that transaction to the appropriate parties. Your friendly neighborhood title person will know what you are talking about when you ask for this document by name. They will typically need some basic information on your transaction such as purchase price, estimated settlement date, loan payoff amount on the Seller's mortgage(s), Seller contribution to Buyer's closing costs, Buyer's loan amount, Buyer's down payment amount, annual property taxes and real estate commissions. Once you provide this information, they can very easily prepare this document for you. (If necessary, feel free to show this information sheet to your title person to help them understand what you want.)

Please recognize that the title company will not have information on the middle section (Holding Costs) and that you need to figure this information with the help of your utility companies, insurance agent, and lender.

Exhibit 4--Remodeling Cost Estimator

SMALL: $10 per SF

PaintPlus = (Paint, Flooring, Minor Landscaping, Some Details, A Good Thorough Cleaning)

MEDIUM: $20 per SF

PaintPlus & Kitchen and Bath(s)

LARGE: $30 per SF

PaintPlus & 2 "Big Ticket" items

EXTRA LARGE: $40 per SF

PaintPlus & 4 "Big Ticket" items

ALWAYS use an inspection contingency in your contract when using estimated repair figures to make your offer!

ALWAYS use a written, detailed bid from a reputable contractor once you have the property under contract to confirm your estimate.

Exhibit 5--Why Your Client Should Work With We Dialogue

"Why your client should work with me"

I buy and sell properties in our community

I pay fair prices

I will give your client a legitimate, written offer within 24 hours of viewing their property

I'm not a real estate agent, so they can save a 6% or 7% commission by selling to me instead of listing with an agent

They don't need to clean, repair, remodel or even clear out the property because I buy in "as is" condition

They don't need to waste time marketing and showing the property, running the risk of listing it with an agent and not having it sell because I'll buy it right now!

I can act quickly- Your client can tell me when they want to close.

I can often pay cash.

Give me a call, I'm happy to work with your clients in solving real estate problems…that is what I do!

Exhibit 6--Why You Should Work With Me Dialogue

"Why you should work with me"

I buy and sell properties in our community

I pay fair prices

I will give you a legitimate, written offer within 24 hours of viewing your property

I'm not a real estate agent, so you can save a 6% or 7% commission by selling to me instead of listing with an agent

You don't need to clean, repair, remodel or even clear out the property because I buy in "as is" condition

You don't need to waste time marketing and showing the property, running the risk of listing it with an agent and not having it sell because I'll buy it right now!

I can act quickly- You tell me when you want to close.

I can often pay cash.

Give me a call, I'm happy to work with you in solving real estate problems…that is what I do!

Exhibit 7--Developing A Relationship With A Title Company or Title Attorney

1.   Ask your agent for a referral to a good Investor-friendly title company

2.   Visit the title company in person with your agent

3.   Have your agent introduce you as one of his/her "Investor clients"

4.   Be sure to ask, "Who should I call if you need information about a property, or to order title work to be done on a property?"

5.   Meet that person and get their contact information (a business card is ideal)

6.   Send them a personal note the next day saying, "It was nice to meet you. I look forward to working with you." or something along those lines

7.   Make it a point to contact them, either in person or by phone at least once a month, just to say hello and keep the relationship going

8.   When you do a deal with them as the closing agent, sent your new friend flowers, a plant, cookies, doughnuts, a personal note, a small gift certificate, etc., as a thank you

The idea of developing and nurturing this relationship may not seem important at first, but you need to recognize the fact that a good relationship with a title company person is like having the key to the information vault for properties in your area.

Exhibit 8--Attorney Letter Example

Property Partners, LLC

March 10, 2014

Dear Mr. Smith,

My name is Tim Bell and I am a local real estate Investor who buys and sells properties within our county and the surrounding areas. Because you work with clients who may be in a situation where they need sell a home, I would like to make you aware of my services such that you might recommend them to your clients should the need arise. Reasons that your clients might want to work with me include:

- I pay fair prices
- I will give your client a legitimate, written offer within 24 hours of viewing their property
- I am not a real estate agent, so your client can save 6% or 7% in commissions by selling to me instead of listing with an agent
- Your client does not need to clean, repair, remodel or even clear out the property; I buy in "as-is" condition
- Your client does not need to waste time marketing and showing their property, running the risk of listing it with an agent and not having it sell because I will buy it now!
- I can act quickly; your client can choose their closing deadline
- I can often pay cash

I am happy to work with you and your clients in solving real estate problems. Please feel free to give me a call if you have any questions, and to pass along my contact information to any of your clients who might benefit from my services.

Sincerely,

Tim Bell

Property Partners, LLC
801-555-1212
www.propertypartners.com

Exhibit 9--Real Estate Purchase Contract

(8 ½" by 14" page size)

OFFER TO PURCHASE
REAL ESTATE

BE IT KNOWN, the undersigned,

_____ (Buyer), offers to
purchase from _____ _____ (Seller),
real estate known as,_____ City/Town of
_____, County of _____, State of
_____, said property more particularly described as:

_____

The purchase price offered is	$
Earnest Money Deposit herewith paid	$
Balance due at closing	$
Total purchase price	$

This offer is conditional upon the following terms:

1. This offer is subject to Buyer obtaining a real estate mortgage for no less than _____ payable over _____ years with interest not to exceed _____% at customary terms with a firm commitment thereto _____days from date hereof.
2. Said property is to be sold free and clear of all encumbrances, by good and marketable title, with full possession to said property available to Buyer at date of closing.
3. The closing shall occur on or before _____, at Buyer's title company or attorney's office, unless such other time and place shall be agreed upon by all parties.
4. In the event that the Buyer does not perform on said agreement, the Seller shall retain the earnest money deposit as their sole remedy under this agreement.
5. This agreement is subject to Buyer's inspection and approval of inspection and an acceptable title report within ___ days of acceptance. Any disapproval will be provided in writing.
6. Buyer and Seller agree to pay normal closing costs as customarily allocated between the parties.
7. Upon acceptance, Buyer shall have the right to immediately begin marketing the property at the Buyer's sole discretion.
8. Upon acceptance, Buyer shall be granted unlimited access to the property for marketing and inspection purposes.
9. Earnest money shall be deposited by Buyer upon acceptance by all parties at _____(insert Title Company Name here)

This offer shall remain in force until _____ o'clock, _____ and if not accepted by said time this offer shall be deemed rescinded and deposits shall be refunded.

_____ Buyer
                                    Date

_____ Buyer
                                    Date

_____

Seller   Date

_____

Seller   Date

Exhibit 10--Wholesaling Clauses

You should seriously consider including the following clauses or their equivalent in all your contracts with Sellers where your intent is to wholesale the property:

1. "Upon acceptance, Buyer shall have the right to immediately begin marketing the property at the Buyer's sole discretion"
2. "Upon acceptance, Buyer shall be granted unlimited access to the property for inspection and marketing purposes"
3. Buyer reserves the unqualified right to transfer the interest in this agreement to any person or entity at his sole discretion.

4. "This agreement is subject to Buyer's inspection and approval of inspection and an acceptable title report within ___ days of acceptance. Any disapproval will be provided in writing."
5. This offer is subject to Buyer obtaining a real estate mortgage for no less than _____ payable over _____ years with interest not to exceed _____% at customary terms with a firm commitment thereto _____days from date hereof
6. "In the event that the Buyer defaults or does not perform on any provision of this agreement for any reason, the Seller shall retain the earnest money deposit as their sole remedy under this agreement"
7. "Earnest money shall be deposited by Buyer upon acceptance by all parties at (insert your Title Company/Title Attorney Name here)"

You should discuss the necessity or advantages of including each of these clauses with your agent if you are having them write the contract for you!

Note: You should not include clauses 3 & 7 in an offer on an REO/Bank Owned property or a Short Sale property. The lender will not accept an assignable contract, and they will want to control where the title work is done.

Exhibit 11--Assignment of Contract Form

ASSIGNMENT OF CONTRACT

_____("Original Buyer") assigns to
_____ ("New Buyer") the Purchase Contract on
_____ between (Original Buyer) and
_____ ("Seller") dated _____. The
Contract is being assigned for the amount of
_____("Assignment Fee").
Upon execution of this Assignment of Contract, New Buyer (Assignee)
hereby agrees to pay Original Buyer (Assignor) a nonrefundable Earnest
Money Deposit in the amount of _____.

-Earnest money to be credited towards agreed upon Assignment Fee at
closing. New Buyer accepts all rights, obligations, and responsibilities
of Purchase Contract executed by Original Buyer and the Seller of said
property.
-New Buyer acknowledges the Earnest Money is nonrefundable except
only under the following circumstances:

1) The Seller declines to sell any time before the expiration of Contract;
and/or
2) The Title cannot be cleared for sale.

Original Buyer
(Assignor)_____Date_____

New Buyer
(Assignee)_____Date_____

Subscribed and sworn to before me this_____ day of
_____, 20__

_____ My commission
expires_____

_____

Notary Public, State of _____

114

Exhibit 12--Affidavit and Memorandum of Agreement Concerning Real Estate
Affidavit and Memorandum of Agreement Concerning Real Estate

State of _____ County of _____

BEFORE ME, the undersigned authority, on this day personally appeared _____, who being first duly sworn, deposes and says that:

1. An agreement for the Purchase and Sale of the real property described in the attached Exhibit "A" was
entered into by and between the Affiant, as Buyer, and
_____, as Seller, on the
_____ day of _____, 20___.
2. The closing of the purchase and sale of said real property, per the terms of the Agreement, is to take place on or before the
_____ day of _____, 20_____.
3. A copy of the agreement for purchase and sale of said real property may be obtained by contacting
_____, whose mailing
address is_____, and whose
telephone number is _____.
Dated this _____ day of _____,
20____.

FURTHER AFFIANT SAYETH NOT.
Signed, sealed and delivered in the presence of:

_____

_____
WITNESS   AFFIANT

_____
WITNESS
Sworn to and subscribed before me this _____ day of _____,
20 __
(Seal) NOTARY PUBLIC STATE OF _____
My commission expires _____

Exhibit 13--Contract to Sell Real Estate

CONTRACT TO SELL REAL ESTATE

BE IT KNOWN, the undersigned,

_____ (Buyer), offers to

purchase from _____

_____ (Seller), real estate known as,

_____ City/Town of _____,

County of _____, State of _____, said property

more particularly described as:

_____

The purchase price offered is	$	
Non-refundable Deposit herewith paid	$	
Balance at closing	$	
Total purchase price	$_____	

This offer is conditional upon the following terms:

1.   This offer is subject to Buyer obtaining a real estate mortgage for no less than _____ payable over _____ years with interest not to exceed _____% at customary terms with a firm commitment thereto _____days from date hereof.

2.   This offer is further subject to Buyer obtaining a satisfactory home inspection report and termite/pest report within _____ days from date hereof.

3.   Owner shall pay broker _____, a commission of $_____ upon closing.

4.   Said property is to be sold free and clear of all encumbrances, by good and marketable title, with full possession to said property available to Buyer at date of closing.

5.   The closing shall occur on or before _____, at Seller's title company or attorney's office, unless such other time and place shall be agreed upon by all parties.

6.   Other terms: Property is sold as is, where is, how is with no warranties expressed or implied. Buyer to pay all closing costs associated with this transaction.

7.   This offer shall remain open until _____ o'clock, _____ and if not accepted by said time this offer shall be deemed rescinded and deposits shall be refunded.

Signed this _____ day of _____

_____
   Buyer   Date

_____

Buyer   Date

_____
Seller   Date

_____
Seller   Date

Subscribed and sworn to before me this _____ day of_____.
_____ My commission expires _____
Notary Public, State of

Exhibit 14--Generic Purchase Contract Addendum

ADDENDUM NUMBER _____ TO REAL ESTATE PURCHASE AGREEMENT

THIS IS AN ADDENDUM to that REAL ESTATE PURCHASE AGREEMENT with an Offer Reference Date of _____, including all prior addenda and counteroffers, between

_____ as Buyer, and
_____ as Seller,

regarding the Property located at_____

The following terms are hereby incorporated as part of the AGREEMENT:

_____
_____
_____
_____

BUYER AND SELLER AGREE THAT THE CONTRACT DEADLINES REFERENCED IN THE AGREEMENT

(CHECK APPLICABLE BOX): [ ] REMAIN UNCHANGED [ ] ARE CHANGED AS FOLLOWS:

To the extent the terms of this ADDENDUM modify or conflict with any provisions of the Agreement, including all prior addenda and counteroffers, these terms shall control. All other terms of the Agreement, including all prior addenda and counteroffers, not modified by this ADDENDUM shall remain the same.

_____

Buyer Signature   Date   Buyer Signature   Date

_____

Seller Signature   Date   Seller Signature   Date

118

Exhibit 15--Cancellation of Contract Form

NOTICE OF CANCELLATION OF REAL ESTATE PURCHASE CONTRACT

DATE:

TO:

RE: Real Estate Purchase Contract with an offer reference date
of _____ between
_____ as Buyer, and
_____ as Seller, for the
property located at

_____

_____ hereinafter referred to as The Contract.

This is to inform you that the Buyer hereby declares The Contract cancelled, null and void. The Property Inspection performed by Buyer indicates that there are several problems with the condition of the property that preclude the Buyers continuing with this purchase.

In accordance with the provisions of The Contract,
_____ will return the Buyer's Earnest Money Deposit. We regret that we were unable to bring this transaction to a successful close. If you have any questions, you may contact me at my office at _____.

Sincerely,

(Your name)

Seller hereby acknowledges Buyer's cancellation of above
referenced Contract

Seller _____ Date _____

Exhibit 16--Sample Wholesale Flyer

Year Built: 1964

4 Total Bedroom(s)

2 Total Bath(s)

Approx. 1507 sq. ft.

Forced Air Heat

Air Conditioning

Oversized 1 Car Garage

Composition Roof

Cinderblock construction

Approx. .23 acres
Fenced Backyard

Needs: Flooring, paint, new
kitchen, new bathrooms,
landscaping

Heat, AC, plumbing and
electrical are all in good
condition.

Exceptional Wholesale Deal!

**After Repair Value $200,000
Repairs $30,000
Buy it today $110,000**

123 Sesame St, Townsville, UT 84123

Timothy Bell 801-555-1212
Property Partners, LLC
www.propertypartners.com

*Property is vacant, key boxed and available for your immediate purchase and renovation.
Call for key box code and view it at your convenience*

Exhibit 17--How to Find Local Foreclosure Auctions

HOW TO FIND LOCAL FORECLOSURE AUCTIONS

- The County Clerk's office or the County Recorder's office in your city or town will have foreclosure notices in their public listings with dates, addresses and times. Before driving all the way down there, check the county website and/or call them on the phone.
- The Sherriff's Department may conduct the foreclosure auction in your area, so contact them and ask.
- Look for a Notice of Default (NOD) or a Notice of Sale (NOS) or Lis Pendens filing in your local newspapers. Typically, for a bank to file a foreclosure, a notice must be published in the newspaper. Check the public notice section of your paper or business journal for a list of trustee sales and auctions.
- Ask the president or other investors at your local real estate investment club(s) where the local foreclosure auctions are held.
- Conduct an online search. Real estate auction services such as RealtyTrac and Foreclosure.com list all of the properties that have been foreclosed and are awaiting auction and often have foreclosure sale locations.
- Check the lenders' websites for foreclosure dates, addresses and times. Some of the banks that include information on foreclosures and auctions include Bank of America, Wells Fargo, IndyMac, HSBC, Suntrust and GMAC.
- Utilize government databases. Homes going into foreclosure that are guaranteed by the government are often sold at auction. You can find those listing through agencies such as Fair Housing Administration (FHA), Veteran's Administration (VA), U.S. Department of Agriculture (USDA) and others

Exhibit 18--Interviewing a Real Estate Agent

The recommended way to conduct this interview is in person, face to face. By visiting their office, you will see what type of agency they associate with. Is it professional and descent, or just a hole in the wall? Most professional agents will associate with professional-looking agencies. Do they have a receptionist, a conference room, computers, fax machines and other basic tools they need to help you? You will also see if they act in a professional manner. Remember that in many instances you will be judged by the company you keep, including your team members. It is always best to work with people who project a professional image, behave in a professional manner and have a positive attitude.

Prior to your visit, call and ask, "Do you work with Investors?" (Most will say yes, but if they have a bunch of reasons why investing won't work in this market, end the conversation and look for someone who is not so negative.) If they say yes, set an appointment to meet with them, "I'd like to meet with you at your office to discuss my business and see if we can work together. When could we meet?"

□ Take notes with you and discuss the following items:

□ I am an Investor and I'm looking for a good, hard working agent for my team.

□ I need someone to represent me from time to time in both buying and selling properties.

□ I will often find properties on my own, but I also want an agent who is willing to help me find properties, write contracts and counter offers, and to negotiate on my behalf.

□ I need you to help me determine which areas in our marketplace are moving and active, and that have relatively low Days On Market. I don't want stagnant neighborhoods where the Days On Market figure is too high (30 to 60 days is best). Also the neighborhoods need to be relatively affordable neighborhoods with modest houses in low to middle income areas, neighborhoods with prices at or below the <u>Median Price</u> for our market for Single Family homes, and within a 30 minute driving radius of my home or office; Neighborhoods that are predominantly 3 Bedroom, 2 Bath houses are typically ideal but we would consider others, too.

☐ I need someone who is very familiar with this area and the state approved purchase contract, and is comfortable working with an Investor who is focused primarily on the numbers, not the "emotional appeal" of a property.

☐ I am looking for properties that I can buy, rehab and resell for a profit.

☐ I have a formula that I use to determine whether or not a property fits my investment plan:

$200,000   After Repair Value (Sales Price after rehab)

-$ 20,000   General Costs (Holding, Carrying, Closing Costs)

-$ 40,000   Profit (20% of ARV)

-$ 30,000   Repair/Rehab costs

$110,000   Maximum Purchase Price

☐ I want someone who is willing to locate properties that have clues that the Seller might be motivated such as "vacant," "fixer upper", "handyman special", "needs work", "needs TLC" etc. and are in moderately priced areas (basically your target area and price range)

☐ Once you locate these properties, I need you to help me analyze the comps and determine what price you would sell it for if it were in top condition (determine ARV)

- [ ] I will review these properties and choose the ones I want to inspect.

- [ ] Once I've looked at them and determined my repair cost, I will let you know what amount I want to offer – in many cases it will be less than the Seller's asking price.

- [ ] Because of that, I'll be asking you to write quite a few of these offers.

- [ ] Does it bother you to submit offers that are less than the Seller's full asking price? (Once again if they object they aren't the agent for you.)

- [ ] I typically work with private lenders or hard money lenders, but I am always on the lookout for new sources of funding for my deals.

- [ ] I would also ask you to give me referrals to other professionals as needed such as a title company, a real estate attorney, an appraiser, an inspector and others.

- [ ] If this all sounds like something that would work for you, we can agree to work together for the next 30 days and see if we have a fit.

If you have an agent that is comfortable with what you've just outlined you don't need more than one agent unless you are working geographical areas that this agent does not cover.

If they want you to sign a Buyer broker agreement, its OK to do so, but you should limit it to properties listed on the MLS and have the agreement valid for no longer than 14-30 days.

Exhibit 19--Business Planning Template

Business Planning for your Real Estate Investment Business

Remember, your business plan does not need to be complex or lengthy. Its purpose is to keep you focused and give you daily guidance and direction for your business and your activities. Read it through every day at the beginning of your day and again at the end of your day. Doing so will help keep your mind focused on your objectives and appropriate activities. Also, it is appropriate to modify it as you and your business evolve over time.

Business Plan Creation Steps

- o Create an Overall Business Plan
- o Work backwards to determine what you need to accomplish
- o Create a Marketing Plan
- o Forecast Profits
- o Run your scenario by an accountant to identify potential tax liabilities
- o Calendar each of your events
- o Follow through!

Create an Overall Business Plan

Make it simple and direct. Answer the following questions:

What do you want to accomplish in the next year?

How much profit do you wish to earn?

How much will you average per property?

What average price range will you be working with?

How extensive is the work that you will do on a property?

(If any)

How long will it take on an average to flip each property? (Combine estimated rehab time with average Days On Market for that neighborhood)

Work backward to determine what you need to accomplish.

Create your One Year objectives first.

Break these objectives down into quarterly, monthly, weekly, daily and also, per project goals.

Assess the viability of these goals, and be willing to revise your objectives.

Be optimistically realistic. In other words push yourself, but don't kill yourself.

Create a Marketing Plan

What are the primary methods you will use to locate properties?

What costs will be involved with each finding strategy?

What methods will you use to market a property for sale?

What are the costs of each of your selling strategies?

What backup methods will you use for finding and selling if your primary methods aren't successful?

Forecast Profits

How much do I plan to earn this year?

Based upon my average profit per property, how many properties will I need to complete during this year?

How much money and credit will this plan require?

How much of my own time will it take to accomplish this?

Is this realistic for my time, money and credit availability?

Do I need to revise my forecasts?

Run your business plan by an accountant to identify potential tax liabilities

You do not want to find yourself at the end of the year with all your money spent and a big tax bill to cover.

Independent business people set aside a portion of their profits to cover taxes.

Meet with an accountant after forecasting to identify your potential tax liability and how much needs to be set aside from each project for taxes.

Discuss Entity structuring techniques and other ideas with your accountant to minimize your tax liability.

Calendar Each of Your Events

Obtain and use a Planning System of some kind: Paper planner, PDA, Smartphone, Online, Outlook, etc. I doesn't matter what you use as long as it works for you and you actually use it!

Schedule all of your business and personal activities in your planning system, leaving some room for unforeseen circumstances and events. You should prioritize your activities to assure that you are accomplishing the most important money making activities and not just plodding along doing easier, less important things.

Professionals always:

Plan their Future and their Today
Prioritize their activities and schedule the "hardest" things first
    Make decisions regarding what is important and what is not
Calendar their events and activities
Go into Action
Constantly Evaluate and Adjust

Commit now to become a professional!

Follow Through

Follow this simple action process throughout your day:

1. Look at your watch to determine the time
2. Look at your calendar in your planning system and determine what you have scheduled to do at the current time
3. If you are not doing what your calendar says you should be doing, immediately stop what you are doing and start doing what your calendar says you should be doing!

Exhibit 20--How to Find the Owner of a Vacant House

Look up the owners name and other information in the county records
- o Netronline.com
- o Dataquick.com
- o Taxnetusa.com
- o Brbpub.com
- o Once you find the owner's name, you may be able to find them on Zabasearch.com

Contact the neighbors, two on the left, two on the right and five across the street; knock on the door, introduce yourself, tell them you are interested in buying their neighbor's vacant home and ask if they know how to reach them.

Mail a letter like the following to the property:

Dear Property Owner

I am a local real estate investor. My company pays cash for properties in any condition.

I noticed your vacant property at _____

If you are interested in selling,
please call my office at 800-555-1212

Call now, we can help you!

Thank you,

Bob Investor

On the envelope write:

PLEASE FORWARD

ADDRESS CORRECTION REQUESTED   Joe Owner

                                     123 Sesame St

                                     Our Town, CA 91111

Call 411 information operator to see if a new phone number has been issued.

Place a bandit sign on the property:

> **CALL ME ABOUT**
> **THIS HOUSE!**
>
> **800-555-1212**

- ✓ If the Seller calls you, ask them if they would consider selling
- ✓ If a Buyer calls you, explain that you haven't finalized the deal on that property but that you anticipate that you will soon and that you will call them soon
- ✓ Also ask a potential Buyer what they are looking for (Bedrooms, bathrooms, area, condition, etc.)

Skip Trace: FindTheSeller.com or other sites

Exhibit 21--We Buy Houses Flyer

WE BUY HOUSES!

Dear Property Owner,

I am a local real estate Investor buying properties in your neighborhood. My partners and I buy properties, fix them up as needed and resell them to nice families, making the neighborhood a better place to live for everyone!

If you are interested in selling or know someone who is please contact my office at 801-555-1212

- ✓ **I pay fair prices**

- ✓ **I will give you a legitimate, written offer within 24 hours of viewing your property**

- ✓ **I'm not a real estate agent, so you can save a 6% or 7% commission by selling to me instead of listing with an agent**

- ✓ **You don't need to clean, repair, remodel or even clear out the property because I buy in "as is" condition**

- ✓ **You don't need to waste time marketing and showing your property, running the risk of listing it with an agent and not having it sell because I'll buy it right now!**

- ✓ **I can act quickly…you tell me when you want to close**

Call me now…I can help you!

Tim Bell, Principle Property Buyer, Property Partners 801-555-1212

Check us out online at propertypartners.com

Acknowledgements

I want to thank and acknowledge Jim Carlson, Cris Cannon and Jeff Spangler for the opportunity they have provided to me to share my knowledge and experience with their students. Because of these three gentlemen's courage, tenacity, entrepreneurship, and outstanding leadership, I have the opportunity to help many, many more people than I ever would have without their organization.

I'm also very grateful for the incredible coaching staff at Advanced Real Estate Education and Zurixx. Just like Tom Cruise's character 'Maverick' in the movie *Top Gun*, I have the privilege of working with the Best of the Best. Greg McCluskey, Bret and Heidi Ehlers, Carter Brown, Liz Higbee, Bud McCluskey, Jessie Wheeler, John Benson, Craig Cornforth, Eric Lloyd, Larry McKinstry, Deborah Price and *Coach* Randy Cochrane; you are my friends and my colleagues, and I'm so thankful for you. I sincerely appreciate all of the wisdom, experience and knowledge that you regularly share with me. Also, thank you to Erin Spainhower and Taylor Ballstaedt, our awesome administrative assistants. I love you like daughters, and your conscientiousness and attention to detail are so inspirational in a working world laden with mediocrity.

Finally, this book wouldn't even exist without my friend, Web guy, covert entrepreneur, tech guru and all around corporate ninja, Mark Sanderson. As a wise man once said, "You don't need to be an MBA, you just need to have one on your team." Thanks Mark for teaching us all the things we never learned in MBA School. Your perspectives and insights are always worthwhile. You have always believed in me. You are my biggest critic and my greatest supporter, and for that I appreciate you more than I can express.

Dedications

To my wonderful wife & eternal companion, Laurie.

You are the beautiful, steady breeze that supports my flight with the eagles.

I know what an angel looks like because I see you every day.

You have all of my love, always and forever.

This is also dedicated to my terrific children & their spouses, of whom I am justifiably proud.

To Tim, Jr., the hardest working man I know

To Brittaney, 'supermodel' mom & multi-talented young lady

To Ian, the most generous person in the world

To Jonathan, who always chooses the right, no matter what

To Caitlin, whose incredible talent makes her my favorite actress of all time

To Victoria, the 'Queen' of our home & the best Esthetician ever

To Emma, our daughter from another mother & our special blessing from God

This is also in remembrance of our late cousin David Silfvast. He had more than his share of challenges in this life, but the freedom of flying upside down always helped him maintain a right side up attitude. He was always happy and smiling because he knew, as we all should know, that God really is our copilot.

About the author

Tim Bell is a Real Estate Investor, Consultant, Trainer, Coach, Mentor, Author, Speaker, Business Manager, Pilot, Geographer, Outdoorsman , Scuba Diver and all around Life Adventurer.

His real estate business has allowed him to do many things in his life. He made his first real estate investment as a 20 year old college student in 1977, and he has experienced firsthand all of the real estate market cycles over the last 40 years.

He lives in the foothills of the Wasatch Mountains in suburban Salt Lake City, Utah with his wife Laurie, his two teenage daughters Victoria and Emma, and his loyal, loving Miniature Fox Terriers, Mollie and Winnie.

Made in the USA
Lexington, KY
29 August 2016